Stories That Could Be True

Stories That Could Be True

New and Collected Poems

by William Stafford

HARPER & ROW, PUBLISHERS

New York, Hagerstown, San Francisco, London

This work contains all the poems in *Traveling Through the Dark*, *The Rescued Year*, *Allegiances*, and *Someday, Maybe* published by Harper & Row, Publishers, Inc., and *West of Your City* published by The Talisman Press.

Grateful acknowledgment is made to the following magazines in which some of the poems first appeared:

The American Poetry Review, *The Atlantic Monthly*, Audience, Ironwood, *Ladies' Home Journal*, *The Land on the Tip of a Hair*, Mikrokosmos, *Modern Poetry Studies*, *The Nation*, New Letters, *The New Review*, Northwest Review, Oregon Rainbow, *PTA Magazine*, Poetry Now, Rapport, *The South Carolina Review*, and *The Virginia Quarterly Review*.

"A Bird Inside a Box" and "Always" originally appeared in *The Hudson Review*.

The poems "Ask Me" and "Slave on the Headland" originally appeared in *The New Yorker*.

"The Burning House" was first published in *The North American Review*.

"This Town: Winter Morning" originally appeared in *Poetry*.

FIRST EDITION

Designed by C. Linda Dingler

Library of Congress Cataloging in Publication Data

Stafford, William Edgar, 1914–
  Stories that could be true.

  Includes index.
  I. Title.
PS3537.T143S7   811'.5'4   77–3775
ISBN 0–06–013988–9

77 78 79 80 81 10 9 8 7 6 5 4 3 2 1

For
My Party the Rain

You again, raindrop,
the same as our first day—and,
yes, it's me again.

Contents

West of Your City (1960)

Traveling Through the Dark (1962)

I. *In Medias Res*

III. *Representing Far Places*

The Rescued Year (1966)

I.

II.

II.

III.

IV.

Someday, Maybe (1973)

I. Motorcycle, Count My Sins

II. *Wind World*

Stories That
Could Be True
1977

I. Believing

Our Story

Remind me again—together we
trace our strange journey, find
each other, come on laughing.
Some time we'll cross where life
ends. We'll both look back
as far as forever, that first day.
I'll touch you—a new world then.
Stars will move a different way.
We'll both end. We'll both begin.

Remind me again.

Always

Inside the trees, where tomorrow
hides along with years, tomorrow
stirs. And there my sisters
never born touch lips to bark
and begin to sing:

Brother of Air, Brother of Sun,
please tell our story, that we
may live in the brief wind.

Wherever I stand I hear the trees
petition so. By listening
I know I'm born. By turning
the forest back toward itself
I live as a friend of trees:

Listen together; be ready.
You may be born. I touch the bark
and call deep as I can:
Part of me.

A Story That Could Be True

If you were exchanged in the cradle and
your real mother died
without ever telling the story
then no one knows your name,
and somewhere in the world
your father is lost and needs you
but you are far away.

He can never find
how true you are, how ready.
When the great wind comes
and the robberies of the rain
you stand on the corner shivering.
The people who go by—
you wonder at their calm.

They miss the whisper that runs
any day in your mind,
"Who are you really, wanderer?"—
and the answer you have to give
no matter how dark and cold
the world around you is:
"Maybe I'm a king."

The Burning House

What does the floor hear—that cousin to earth?
A little tap, determined. Coming? No one.
Then a chair scrapes, and everywhere thunder.

Now everywhere has my home, reclaimed
earth, dust: it crossed borders, crept
under the praying emperor's knee.

Oh mansion all windows now!
Deepest and widest home—the swallows' barn,
or—"Fish, let me shake your fin."

My home is a home for all. Come in.

Wovoka's Witness

1

The people around me,
they meet me. Often they will talk, and
listen. They give regard, and I
to them. A few can't respond. Their faces
are dead. When these people meet me
and fail, I am sorry for them. For them
it is already the end of the world.

2

You people, my eyes are taking your picture
and putting it on a ribbon that winds
inside my head. My ears capture your voice
to hold for lonely years. My hands
have a game: "Are you there? Are you there?"
Remember? We play that game
again and again.

5

3

My people, now it is time
for us all to shake hands with the rain.
It's a neighbor, lives here all winter.
Talkative, yes. It will tap late
at night on your door and stay there
gossiping. It goes away without a goodby
leaving its gray touch on old wood.
Where the rain's giant shoulders make a silver
robe and shake it, there are wide places.
There are cliffs where the rain leans, and
lakes that give thanks for miles
into the mountains. We owe the rain
a pat on the back—barefoot, it has walked
with us with its silver passport all over the world.

4

My own people, now listen—if we fail
all the trees in the forest will cease
to exist, or only their ghosts will stand
there fooling everyone. The wind will
pretend and the mountains will step back
through their miles of drenching fake rain.
Listen now—we must let the others make movies
of us. Be brave. Charge into their cameras
and bring them alive. They too
may dream. They too may find
the ghost dance, and be real.

Things in the Wild Need Salt

Of the many histories, Earth tells only one—
Earth misses many things people tell about,
like maybe there are earthquakes that we should have had,
or animals that know more love than God ever felt.

And we need these things: things in the wild need salt.

6

Once in a cave a little bar of light
fell into my hand. The walls leaned over me.
I carried it outside to let the stars look;
they peered in my hand. Stars are like that.

Do not be afraid—I no longer carry it.
But when I see a face now, splinters of that light
fall and won't go out, no matter how faint
the buried star shines back there in the cave.

It is in the earth wherever I walk.
It is in the earth wherever I walk.

Blackbirds

One day we sang,
"The wind is coming along."
And where we sang, it came.

Then we flew that country, green
grass, black fields;
wo olid it by miloo paot our oyoo.

By miles it grandly
came below the edge of our wings,
borne up by thousands of songs
    from throats of Northland birds.

We tilted and found our
lake, a world with reeds.
Today we sing it all back at the sky.

Some Evening

In the form of mist, from under a stone,
a soul comes forth and lingers along
the ground to clasp your foot:
"Oh happy being, where can my body be found?"

You remember a ruined face you saw
lost in the passing crowd: this low wraith
is the other half of such a bereft wanderer
never at rest, always alone.

You happy beings, watch every face for those
you pass caught in the midst of life
by some horror, their souls gone dim, cursed
or unlucky, exiled under a stone.

Heard Under a Tin Sign at the Beach

I am the wind. Long ago
high in the mountains I had a home.
Three brothers before me set forth
quarreling, and I fell away silently
in a swoop on the steep side.

I am looking under leaves for someone,
examining everything in the world,
combing fields. When my brothers meet
we wrestle out over the sea
and they break away. I love their faces.

When you meet me and bow
I remember all our meetings,
the joy. Now in parting, here
is my embrace. There will be
these times again, no matter how far.

8

Accountability

Cold nights outside the taverns in Wyoming
pickups and big semi's lounge idling, letting their
haunches twitch now and then in gusts of powder snow,
their owners inside for hours, forgetting as well
as they can the miles, the circling plains, the still town
that connects to nothing but cold and space and a few
stray ribbons of pavement, icy guides to nothing
but bigger towns and other taverns that glitter and wait:
Denver, Cheyenne.

Hibernating in the library of the school on the hill
a few pieces by Thomas Aquinas or Saint Teresa
and the fragmentary explorations of people like Alfred
North Whitehead crouch and wait amid research folders
on energy and military recruitment posters glimpsed
by the hard stars. The school bus by the door, a yellow
mound, clangs open and shut as the wind finds a loose
door and worries it all night, letting the hollow
students count off and break up and blow away
over the frozen ground.

A Message from the Wanderer

Today outside your prison I stand
and rattle my walking stick: Prisoners, listen;
you have relatives outside. And there are
thousands of ways to escape.

Years ago I bent my skill to keep my
cell locked, had chains smuggled to me in pies,
and shouted my plans to jailers;
but always new plans occurred to me,
or the new heavy locks bent hinges off,
or some stupid jailer would forget
and leave the keys.

Inside, I dreamed of constellations—
those feeding creatures outlined by stars,
their skeletons a darkness between jewels,
heroes that exist only where they are not.

Thus freedom always came nibbling my thought,
just as—often, in light, on the open hills—
you can pass an antelope and not know
and look back, and then—even before you see—
there is something wrong about the grass.
And then you see.

That's the way everything in the world is waiting.

Now—these few more words, and then I'm
gone: Tell everyone just to remember
their names, and remind others, later, when we
find each other. Tell the little ones
to cry and then go to sleep, curled up
where they can. And if any of us get lost,
if any of us cannot come all the way—
remember: there will come a time when
all we have said and all we have hoped
will be all right.

There will be that form in the grass.

II. Being Good

Look

From my head this bubble labeled "Love"
goes up. It is in color, like a balloon. I am
thinking it. And my hair is crowded like that
often. I remember streams of bubbles

10

when I walk—they go bouncing off through the trees.
And once my neck got stretched on Main by a big
ballooning thought when the mayor's daughter suddenly
turned and took me for someone else. This
bend when I listen, even today, is that romance
that flared and went out so fast that no one knew.
Any time, any time, big ideas come along.
This bubble here is always ready, for you.

Song Now

Guitar string is.
Everything else can wait.
Silence puts a paw
wherever the music rests.

All we have is need.
Before and After are falling.
Now is going away.
Sound is the only sky.

Guitar string is:
it can save this place.

At the Playground

Away down deep and away up high,
a swing drops you into the sky.
Back, it draws you away down deep,
forth, it flings you in a sweep
all the way to the stars and back
—Goodby, Jill; Goodby, Jack:
shuddering climb wild and steep,
away up high, away down deep.

Artist, Come Home

Remember how bright it is,
the old rabbitbush by the hall light?

One of the blackberry vines has
reached all the way to the clothesline.

There isn't any way to keep
the kitchen window from tapping.

The tea kettle had one of its meditative
spells yesterday.

I am thinking again of that old
plan—breakfast first, then the newspaper.

They say maybe they won't have
that big war this year after all.

A frog is living under the
back step.

Wild Horse Lore

Downhill, any gait will serve.

It tastes good—a little snow
on old hay.

A stylish mane finds
the wind.

The world, and enough grass—
we don't need the cavalry
any more.

Fictions

They make a song for their dogs, up North,
four-letter words only, the kind
real dogs can use, bark-bark, woof-
woof, and so on—you know;
and every night they go to call
the big one—"Pavlov! Pavlov!"—
strictly home on obedient paths in the snow.

A song like that, or any temporary spot,
pitched cunningly to our minds, can
open the world again and again, lead
easily through our city the wildest stories,
make beautiful—young or old—all the faces,
and send us out to rejoice, wild even in
autumn, under the free-spending sycamores.

My Party the Rain

Loves upturned faces, laves everybody,
applauds tennis courts, pavements; its fingers
ache and march through the forest numbering
limbs, animals, Boy Scouts; it recognizes
every face, the blind, the criminal,
beggar or millionaire, despairing child,
minister cloaked; it finds all the dead
by their stones or mounds, or their deeper listening
for the help of such rain, a census that cares
as much as any party, neutral in politics.

It proposes your health, Governor, at the Capitol;
licks every stone, likes the shape of our state.
Let wind in high snow this year
legislate its own mystery: our lower winter
rain feathers in over miles of trees
to explore. A cold, cellophane layer,

silver wet, it believes what it touches,
and goes on, persuading one thing at a time,
fair, clear, honest, kind—
a long session, Governor. Who knows the end?

On a Church Lawn

Dandelion cavalry, light little saviors,
baffle the wind, they ride so light.
They surround a church and outside the window
utter their deaf little cry: "If you listen
well, music won't have to happen."

After service they depart singly
to mention in the world their dandelion faith:
"God is not big; He is right."

Ducks Down in the Meadow

Stars, it is the end.
Ducks begin to wake—they'll never
walk as well as we do. It's
uphill to the water. Air loves
a quack. Other ponds or rivers
can't be as good as this.
It is all right to shiver your tail
and holler. No one will ever
bend a neck like Mama. Feet are to feel
earthquakes before they come,
and after they are gone. You won't
get to Heaven or see times again like this
till you've dived a wave, seen
dawn arrive in gold, there along the crest,
the way it does for us.

14

Another Old Guitar

For years I was tuned a few notes too high—
I don't see how I could stand it!
You can imagine the strain, hours of
'teen parties, and then beach trips with
"Michael rowed the boat . . ." and later
the marches in all weather singing "We
shall overcome. . . ." Then I moved on.

Now I play in an Eskimo band in Alaska.
I'll never get back outside, through storms;
I dream of returning under a river, breathing
through a straw, carried where the current
hides itself by being just the river. . . .
No. We play in the tin buildings
for the Air Force, and always end with
a relaxed little number the band call
their national anthem: "Somebody, Maybe."

III. Learning to Live in the World

Slave on the Headland

When they brought me here from the north island
my mother stayed alive but I didn't tell
where she lay hidden, headland of spray
waiting for canoes farther north that would come.
For years in gull voices I heard echoes
of dying that day, and my father spoke then,
wind counseling where to turn my eyes
when captors talked about returning to the island.
Gradually I learned this wasn't to be.
Now they call me "The Silent." My work
takes me where gulls wander all day,

and wind. I bend over, listening far,
but also at home here: this island is one
of the mountains connected with all the earth
my father told me about, and he still wanders
calling together the scattered pieces
over my bent head and the wide sea.

One Life

Pascal glanced at infinity;
infinity stared at him:
the world spun like a balloon,
never the same again.

Pascal balanced with care
the blade of the mind all his life:
aghast, he saw Montaigne
play mumblety peg with that knife.

Pascal fell out of a carriage;
his thoughts fell into the sky:
his heart multiplied reasons
as he began to die.

Nothing was left but pain,
bigger than the world, at the end:
of all Port Royal and the Church,
and the King, God was the only friend.

The Little Girl by the Fence at School

Grass that was moving found all shades of brown,
moved them along, flowed autumn away
galloping southward where summer had gone.

16

And that was the morning someone's heart stopped
and all became still. A girl said, "Forever?"
And the grass: "Yes. Forever." While the sky—

The sky—the sky—the sky.

Growing Up

One of my wings beat faster,
I couldn't help it—
the one away from the light.

It hurt to be told all the time
how I loved that terrible flame.

At the Un-National Monument Along the Canadian Border

This is the field where the battle did not happen,
where the unknown soldier did not die.
This is the field where grass joined hands,
where no monument stands,
and the only heroic thing is the sky.

Birds fly here without any sound,
unfolding their wings across the open.
No people killed—or were killed—on this ground
hallowed by neglect and an air so tame
that people celebrate it by forgetting its name.

Surviving a Poetry Circuit

My name is Old Mortality—mine is the hand
that carves the tombstones all over the land.

When you talk, I listen. My ears are keen—
not for what you say, but for what the lies may mean.

If you look away when those around you are hurt,
I bend for my chisel and pick it up from the dirt,

And for every evil you do I cut one more line
across the face of a rock at the end of time.

To make all clean and clear, I tap on your tombstone,
lest moss take all our names when Old Mortality's gone.

One of Your Lives

One of your lives, hurt by the mere sight of
cold, you pulled away to tremble
the drama, too afraid to be warm.
But now, this one, hurtled past
zero and still falling, you are clamped where
no shiver can catch up, imagination
left behind by blurred, actual cold
exploding inside your body.

Remember how easy it was, being
afraid?—you look back and yearn
for the distance of terror, how aesthetic
fear was. These fluttering hands now press
hard fingerprints onto a freezing
face, and suddenly you know why it moves,
why you feel it so well:

It is yours.

18

Ask Me

Some time when the river is ice ask me
mistakes I have made. Ask me whether
what I have done is my life. Others
have come in their slow way into
my thought, and some have tried to help
or to hurt: ask me what difference
their strongest love or hate has made.

I will listen to what you say.
You and I can turn and look
at the silent river and wait. We know
the current is there, hidden; and there
are comings and goings from miles away
that hold the stillness exactly before us.
What the river says, that is what I say.

A Bird Inside a Box

A bird inside a box, a box will
sing. You put it in a window
for the sun—at first the song
hides, then it calls to everyone.

Every day let loose again, those
faithful notes, they're gone, they're
gone so many deathless vows—
and songs—and friends.

Young, you tremble. Old, you do
again, in fear. Between, a rock
inside, you hold the wild bird still
like this, in here, in here.

IV. Whispered into the Ground

The Moment Again

In breath, where kingdoms hide,
one little turn at the end
is king, again, again, again.
That moment hides in the breath
to be time's king: others may vaunt;
that one will never pretend.

The moment that hides in the breath
to be king when kingdoms end
waits when you dial a number:
wire hums; day blooms; light
breaks into a cave; a faint
calm voice floats forward—

You remember a screen door slam,
a scribble of sound, other days. . . .
Then the moment that hides in the breath
to be time's king moves away,
alive in its wave, never in haste,
as you say "Hello" to whoever it is,

Waiting again.

Apologia Pro Vita Sua

As I traveled the earth I heard
about stars. With my feet I told
fields where I wanted to live.
My talk would pretend, but the words
hid a song. From far off

a telescope followed my dance.
I watched the world: it was
only a play. But my mother
cried, because it was love.

Broken Home

Here is a cup left empty in their
kitchen, a brim of that silent air
all the cold mornings, all the cold years.

Here's an old jacket that held a scared heart
too loud for this house, hurt
in its pocket, wanting out.

How alone is this house!—an unreeled
phone dangling down a hall
that never really could lead to tomorrow.

Islands

There could be an island
no one ever finds,
and islands you desecrate
even by thinking them—
so delicately they cling
to their thin horizon.

You people who command things near,
who rule by forgetting islands,
sure, that's the way to success,
and fashion has a shop
on the way home from betrayal,
but one should never neglect
anything, anything.

Sitting Up Late

Beyond silence, on the other side merging
deep in the night, a wolf call lifted slowly
teasing farther than air extended,
thrilling into one pinpoint
across the ice.

The rest of my life
there never comes a simple feeling,
or warmth, or success, for always mingled
in the world is what I knew then
crystalized into a dark faith,
absolute,
between one breath and the next.

One of the Years

Hat pulled low at work,
I saw the branding iron
take the first snowflake.

Whenever It Is

You stand in the magnet's embrace. What
comes near tingles before the crush.
The magnet waits again. Far off
there's a call. You are the only one
who hears. It is the spin of the world.

All around where you stand, the fields,
the trees, and the sky above them begin

to tense, become even more what they were.
People have died of this. Their graves
in summer grass in the country have shocked you.

Your eyes begin to turn back, and gradually
the light in the sky is the light of the sun.
The trees lean, straighten. You put
your hand on the ground. It is dirt again.
Time is back in its cage. It is today.

A Bridge Begins in the Trees

In an owl cry, night became real night;
from that owl cry night came
on the nerve. I felt the shock
and rolled into the dark upon my feet
listening. There was no wind.

Among the firs my fire was almost out;
I heard the lake shore tapping, then
what was no wind, a cry
within the owl cry, behind the cross
of dark the mountain made.

"Honest love will come near fire," I cried,
"and counts all partway friendship a despair."
(For that night sound had struck a nerve,
a crazybone; or some old crag had lapsed,
or just the fire had died.)

My voice went echoing, inventing response
around the world for all of our greatest need,
the longest arc, toward Friend, from All Alone.
For that brief tenure my old faith
sang again along the bone.

Peace Walk

We wondered what our walk should mean,
taking that un-march quietly;
the sun stared at our signs—"Thou shalt not kill."

Men by a tavern said, "Those foreigners . . ."
to a woman with a fur, who turned away—
like an elevator going down, their look at us.

Along a curb, their signs lined across,
a picket line stopped and stared
the whole width of the street, at ours: "Unfair."

Above our heads the sound truck blared—
by the park, under the autumn trees—
it said that love could fill the atmosphere:

Occur, slow the other fallout, unseen,
on islands everywhere—fallout, falling
unheard. We held our poster up to shade our eyes.

At the end we just walked away;
no one was there to tell us where to leave the signs.

This Town: Winter Morning

This town has a spire,
sun on one side—fire:
morning starts to glow.

What the sun touched glistens.
Every shadow listens—
long lines on the snow.

24

When this town was newer
morning light was truer:
heroes of the dawn

Started, pulled their shadows
far across the meadows,
broke free and were gone.

Any night we hear them
when the sunlight leaves them:
by moonlight they return—

     "I'm the dog of silver."
     "I'm the long-lost soldier."
     And softly where God guards the dust—
     "I'm the girl who burned."

Whispered into the Ground

Where the wind ended and we came down
it was all grass. Some of us found
a way to the dirt—easy and rich
When it rained, we grew, except
those of us caught up in leaves, not touching
earth, which always starts things.
Often we sent off our own
just as we'd done, floating that
wonderful wind that promised new land.

Here now spread low, flat on this
precious part of the world, we miss
those dreams and the strange old places
we left behind. We quietly wait.
The wind keeps telling us something
we want to pass on to the world:
Even far things are real.

West of
Your City
1960

Midwest

West of your city into the fern
sympathy, sympathy rolls the train
all through the night on a lateral line
where the shape of game fish tapers down
from a reach where cougar paws touch water.

Corn that the starving Indians held
all through moons of cold for seed
and then they lost in stony ground
the gods told them to plant it in—
west of your city that corn still lies.

Cocked in that land tactile as leaves
wild things wait crouched in those valleys
west of your city outside your lives
in the ultimate wind, the whole land's wave,
Come west and see; touch these leaves.

One Home

Mine was a Midwest home—you can keep your world.
Plain black hats rode the thoughts that made our code.
We sang hymns in the house; the roof was near God.

The light bulb that hung in the pantry made a wan light,
but we could read by it the names of preserves—
outside, the buffalo grass, and the wind in the night.

A wildcat sprang at Grandpa on the Fourth of July
when he was cutting plum bushes for fuel,
before Indians pulled the West over the edge of the sky.

To anyone who looked at us we said, "My friend";
liking the cut of a thought, we could say "Hello."
(But plain black hats rode the thoughts that made our code.)

The sun was over our town; it was like a blade.
Kicking cottonwood leaves we ran toward storms.
Wherever we looked the land would hold us up.

Ceremony

On the third finger of my left hand
under the bank of the Ninnescah
a muskrat whirled and bit to the bone.
The mangled hand made the water red.

That was something the ocean would remember:
I saw me in the current flowing through the land,
rolling, touching roots, the world incarnadined,
and the river richer by a kind of marriage.

While in the woods an owl started quavering
with drops like tears I raised my arm.
Under the bank a muskrat was trembling
with meaning my hand would wear forever.

In that river my blood flowed on.

In the Deep Channel

Setting a trotline after sundown
if we went far enough away in the night
sometimes up out of deep water
would come a secret-headed channel cat,

Eyes that were still eyes in the rush of darkness,
flowing feelers noncommittal and black,
and hidden in the fins those rasping bone daggers,
with one spiking upward on its back.

We would come at daylight and find the line sag,
the fishbelly gleam and the rush on the tether:
to feel the swerve and the deep current
which tugged at the tree roots below the river.

At the Salt Marsh

Those teal with traveling wings
had done nothing to us but they were meat
and we waited for them with killer guns
in the blind deceitful in the rain.

They flew so arrowy till when they fell
where the dead grass bent flat and wet
that I looked for something after nightfall
to come tell me why it was all right.

I touched the soft head with eyes gone
and felt through the feathers all the dark
while we steamed our socks by the fire
and stubborn flame licked the bark.

Still I wonder, out through the raw blow
out over the rain that levels the reeds,
how broken parts can be wrong but true.
I scatter my asking. I hold the duck head.

31

Hail Mary

Cedars darkened their slow way
over the gravel in town graveyards
in places we lived—Wichita, or Haven.

By themselves, withdrawn, secret little shadows
in their corners by the iron gate,
they bowed to the wind that noticed them,

Branches bending to touch the earth;
or night raised them to block the sun
with a thousand utterly weak little hands,

Reciting. They say candle-vigilant woods
in high Arizona swirl twisting upward
out of red dust miles of such emphasis,

Like them, dark by dark by dark.

Circle of Breath

The night my father died the moon shone on the snow.
I drove in from the west; mother was at the door.
All the light in the room extended like a shadow.
Truant from knowing, I stood where the great dark fell.

There was a time before, something we used to tell—
how we parked the car in a storm and walked into a field
to know how it was to be cut off, out in the dark alone.
My father and I stood together while the storm went by.

A windmill was there in the field giving its little cry
while we stood calm in ourselves, knowing we could go home.
But I stood on the skull of the world the night he died, and knew
that I leased a place to live with my white breath.

Truant no more, I stepped forward and learned his death.

Listening

My father could hear a little animal step,
or a moth in the dark against the screen,
and every far sound called the listening out
into places where the rest of us had never been.

More spoke to him from the soft wild night
than came to our porch for us on the wind;
we would watch him look up and his face go keen
till the walls of the world flared, widened.

My father heard so much that we still stand
inviting the quiet by turning the face,
waiting for a time when something in the night
will touch us too from that other place.

A Visit Home

In my sixties I will buy a hat
and wear it as my father did.
At the corner of Central and Main.

There may be flowers by the courthouse windows
and rich offices where those town-men
cheated him in 1929.

For calculation has exploded—
boom, war, oilwells, and, God!
the slow town-men eyes and blue-serge luck.

But at the door of the library I'll lean my cane
and put my hand on buckshot
books: Dewey, Parrington, Veblen . . .

There will be many things in the slant of my hat
at the corner of Central and Main.

The Farm on the Great Plains

A telephone line goes cold;
birds tread it wherever it goes.
A farm back of a great plain
tugs an end of the line.

I call that farm every year,
ringing it, listening, still;
no one is home at the farm,
the line gives only a hum.

Some year I will ring the line
on a night at last the right one,
and with an eye tapered for braille
from the phone on the wall

I will see the tenant who waits—
the last one left at the place;
through the dark my braille eye
will lovingly touch his face.

"Hello, is Mother at home?"
No one is home today.
"But Father—he should be there."
No one—no one is here.

"But you—are you the one . . . ?"
Then the line will be gone
because both ends will be home:
no space, no birds, no farm.

My self will be the plain,
wise as winter is gray,
pure as cold posts go
pacing toward what I know.

Far West

Walking West

Anyone with quiet pace who
walks a gray road in the West
may hear a badger underground where
in deep flint another time is

Caught by flint and held forever,
the quiet pace of God stopped still.
Anyone who listens walks on
time that dogs him single file,

To mountains that are far from people,
the face of the land gone gray like flint.
Badgers dig their little lives there,
quiet-paced the land lies gaunt,

The railroad dies by a yellow depot,
town falls away toward a muddy creek.
Badger-gray the sod goes under
a river of wind, a hawk on a stick.

A Survey

Down in the Frantic Mountains
they say a canyon winds
crammed with hysterical water
hushed by placid sands.

They tried to map that country,
sent out a field boot crew,
but the river surged at night
and ripped the map in two.

35

So they sent out wildcats, printed
with intricate lines of fur,
to put their paws with such finesse
the ground was unaware.

Now only the wildcats know it,
patting a tentative paw,
soothing the hackles of ridges,
pouring past rocks and away.

The sun rakes that land each morning;
the mountains buck and scream.
By night the wildcats pad by
gazing it quiet again.

Our People

Under the killdeer cry
our people hunted all day
graying toward winter, their lodges
thin to the north wind's edge.

Watching miles of marsh grass
take the supreme caress,
they looked out over the earth,
and the north wind felt like the truth.

Fluttering in that wind
they stood there on the world,
clenched in their own lived story
under the killdeer cry.

In the Oregon Country

From old Fort Walla Walla and the Klickitats
to Umpqua near Port Orford, stinking fish tribes
massacred our founders, the thieving whites.

Chief Rotten Belly slew them at a feast;
Kamiakin riled the Snakes and Yakimas;
all spurted arrows through the Cascades west.

Those tribes became debris on their own lands:
Captain Jack's wide face above the rope,
his Modoc women dead with twitching hands.

The last and the most splendid, Nez Percé
Chief Joseph, fluttering eagles through Idaho,
dashed his pony-killing getaway.

They got him. Repeating rifles bored at his head,
and in one fell look Chief Joseph saw the game
out of that spiral mirror all explode.

Back of the Northwest map their country goes,
mountains yielding and hiding fold on fold,
gorged with yew trees that were good for bows.

The Gun of Billy the Kid

When they factoried Billy's gun
and threaded it on that string
that ended in far hearts,
the quitting bell rang.

From a gunshop with walls honeycombed
mild as church sunlight
with promises for the soul
the gun went out to hunt.

That line the gun barrel followed
wavering for years then trued
went strangely devious on Sunday,
tugging at its pool of blood.

Nosing miles of promise
the front sight could find its game
and rest at point with no doubt—
this the round world confirms,

But over the wall of the world
there spills each lonely soul,
and snapping a gun won't help
the journey we all have to go:

In the iron of every day
stars can come through the sky,
and we can turn on the light
and be saved before we die.

Now I once handled firearms
but I handed them back again,
being a pacifist—
then why do I sing this song?

Because, of all the lost,
only the sign of the cross
can bring a killer home,
and Billy the Kid was one,

And Smith and Wesson, who helped,
and singers and story-tellers,
kids in the vacant lots—
all careless hearty fellows.

I follow this, light and strong—
this belief men treat like smoke deer—
through a world like our Southwest
with its monotony, distance, and power.

Billy the Kid was game,
but his game was murder in life:
to know, to see, to save—
for these do good men strive.

And I say my story is true
and is about God and is well;
I tell it the way it came to me,
as one of the truths to tell.

Weather Report

Light wind at Grand Prairie, drifting snow.
Low at Vermilion, forty degrees of frost.
Lost in the Barrens, hunting over spines of ice,
the great sled dog Shadow is running for his life.

All who hear—in your wide horizon of thought
caught in this cold, the world all going gray—
pray for the frozen dead at Yellow Knife.
These words we send are becoming parts of their night.

Vacation

One scene as I bow to pour her coffee:—

>   Three Indians in the scouring drouth
>   huddle at a grave scooped in the gravel,
>   lean to the wind as our train goes by.
>   Someone is gone.
>   There is dust on everything in Nevada.

I pour the cream.

Willa Cather

Far as the night goes, brittle as the stars,
the icy plain pours, a wolf wind over it,
till white in the south plunge peaks with their cold names,
curled like wreaths of stone with blizzard plumes.
In the highway shed at Greybull the workers pause
and hear that wind biting their fences down,
scouring the land, as in early days the Sioux
with winter riding their backs in the folds of their robes
fled the White Father toward the Bitter Roots.

Over that shaking grass a thousand miles
where Spanish Johnny sang to the man he killed,
Nebraska, stretching, touched a continent
trying from the rock of Quebec to Santa Fe
for a certain humble manner of meeting the days:
cedars repeated themselves over the scarred ground,
surrounding with patience the Archbishop's garden;
a badger dug a den wisely; down in Shimerda's
dugout a face turned toward mesas and some still town.

That land required some gesture: conciliation.
A steady look from a professor's house
made the space of America slide into view
to press against the cheekbones all its wind
that carved the land for miles, and in the wind
an old man was calling a language he barely knew,
calling for human help in the wide land, calling
"Te-éach, te-éach my Ántonia"—
into all that silence and the judgment of the sky.

Small Item

A tumbleweed that was trying,
all along through Texas, failed
and became a wraith one winter
in a fence beyond Las Vegas.

All you fortunate in this town
walking, turning, being so sure,
and catching yourselves before ruin,
graceful and intent on your own—

In the space between your triumphs,
the tumbleweed, missing and trying,
flickered out there, haphazard, with grace too,
flared beautifully wasted at random.

At the Bomb Testing Site

At noon in the desert a panting lizard
waited for history, its elbows tense,
watching the curve of a particular road
as if something might happen.

It was looking at something farther off
than people could see, an important scene
acted in stone for little selves
at the flute end of consequences.

There was just a continent without much on it
under a sky that never cared less.
Ready for a change, the elbows waited.
The hands gripped hard on the desert.

Lore

Dogs that eat fish edging tidewater die—
some kind of germ, or too much vitamin.
Indian dogs ate copper for a cure;
a penny will save a spaniel that ate salmon.

113115

On the shore beachcombers find a float
of glass the Japanese used on a net
that broke away deep over the side of the world
and slid blue here on the beach as a gift.

Pieces of driftwood turn into time
and wedge among rocks the breakers pound.
Finding such wrought-work you wonder if the tide
brings in something else when the sun goes down.

By the Snake River

*"There is, in fact, being demanded from the will
that which our conditions of life refuse to allow."*
—ALBERT SCHWEITZER

Something sent me out in these desert places
to this apparition river among the rocks
because what I tried to carry in my hands
was all spilled from jostling when I went
among the people to be one of them.

This river started among such mountains
that I look up to find those valleys
where intentions were before they flowed
in the kind of course the people would allow
where I was a teacher, a son, a father, a man.

Hills lean away from the loss of this river
while it draws on lakes that hang still among clouds
for its variable journey among scars and lava,
exiled for that time from all green for days
and seeking along sandbars of bereavement at night.

This river is what tawny is and loneliness,
and it comes down with a wilderness of power
now and then begging along a little green island
with lush water grass among the rocks
where I have watched it and its broken shells.

The desert it needs possesses too my eyes
whenever they become most themselves to find
what I am, among sights given by chance
while I seek among rocks, while the deep sturgeon move
in this water I lift pouring through my hands.

The Fish Counter at Bonneville

Downstream they have killed the river and built a dam;
by that power they wire to here a light:
a turbine strides high poles to spit its flame
at this flume going down. A spot glows white
where an old man looks on at the ghosts of the game
in the flickering twilight—deep dumb shapes that glide.

So many Chinook souls, so many Silverside.

Sauvies Island

Some years ago I first hunted on Sauvies Island.
Wide, low, marshy—it was in the way
for explorers, except when they wanted game.
Now it is held by spare-time hunters like me.

What do we gain on Sauvies Island? I can tell you
in the space of this one little block: neglect.
We don't expect or give anything—we just go hunting.
It's a wild spot, and little is expected.

Of late I have been very successful.
My friends and family count more and more on me.
On that first trip I shot one duck;
my partner was deservedly surprised when I let him eat half.

My life has become counted on by too many nice people;
going back I hunt little surprises, and Sauvies Islands.

Watching the Jet Planes Dive

We must go back and find a trail on the ground
back of the forest and mountain on the slow land;
we must begin to circle on the intricate sod.
By such wild beginnings without help we may find
the small trail on through the buffalo-bean vines.

We must go back with noses and the palms of our hands,
and climb over the map in far places, everywhere,
and lie down whenever there is doubt and sleep there.
If roads are unconnected we must make a path,
no matter how far it is, or how lowly we arrive.

We must find something forgotten by everyone alive,
and make some fabulous gesture when the sun goes down
as they do by custom in little Mexico towns
where they crawl for some ritual up a rocky steep.
The jet planes dive; we must travel on our knees.

The Move to California

1

The Summons in Indiana

In the crept hours on our street
(repaired by snow that winter night)
from the west an angel of blown newspaper
was coming toward our house out of the dark.

Under all the far streetlights
and along all the near housefronts
silence was painting what it was given
that in that instant I was to know.

Starting up, mittened by sleep, I thought
of the sweeping stars and the wide night,
remembering as well as I could the hedges
back home that minister to comprehended fields—

And other such limits to hold the time near,
for I felt among strangers on a meteor
trying to learn their kind of numbers
to scream together in a new kind of algebra.

That night the angel went by in the dark,
but left a summons: Try farther west.
And it did no good to try to read it again:
there are things you cannot learn through manyness.

2

Glimpsed on the Way

Think of the miles we left,
and then the one slow cliff
coming across the north,
and snow.

From then on, wherever north was,
hovering over us
always it would go,
everywhere.

I wander that desert yet
whenever we draw toward night.
Somewhere ahead that cliff
still goes.

3

At the Summit

Past the middle of the continent—
wheatfields turning in God's hand
green to pale to yellow,
like the season gradual—
we approached the summit
prepared to face the imminent
map of all our vision,
the sudden look at new land.

As we stopped there, neutral,
standing on the Great Divide,
alpine flora, lodgepole pine
fluttering down on either side—
a little tree just three feet high
shared our space between the clouds,
opposing all the veering winds.
Unhurried, we went down.

4

Springs Near Hagerman

Water leaps from lava near Hagerman,
piles down riverward over rock
reverberating tons of exploding shock
        out of that stilled world.

We halted there once. In that cool
we drank, for back and where we had to go
lay our jobs and Idaho,
        lying far from such water.

At work when I vision that sacred land—
the vacation of mist over its rock wall—
I go blind with hope. That plumed fall
        is bright to remember.

46

5

Along Highway 40

Those who wear green glasses through Nevada
travel a ghastly road in unbelievable cars
and lose pale dollars
under violet hoods when they park at gambling houses.

I saw those martyrs—all sure of their cars in the open
and always believers in any handle they pulled—
wracked on an invisible cross
and staring at a green table.

While the stars were watching
I crossed the Sierras in my old Dodge
letting the speedometer measure God's kindness,
and slept in the wilderness on the hard ground.

6

Written on the Stub of the First Paycheck

Gasoline makes game scarce.
In Elko, Nevada, I remember a stuffed wildcat
someone had shot on Bing Crosby's ranch.
I stood in the filling station
breathing fumes and reading the snarl of a map.

There were peaks to the left so high
they almost got away in the heat;
Reno and Las Vegas were ahead.
I had promise of the California job,
and three kids with me.

It takes a lot of miles to equal one wildcat
today. We moved into a housing tract.
Every dodging animal carries my hope in Nevada.
It has been a long day, Bing.
Wherever I go is your ranch.

Outside

Bi-Focal

Sometimes up out of this land
a legend begins to move.
Is it a coming near
of something under love?

Love is of the earth only,
the surface, a map of roads
leading wherever go miles
or little bushes nod.

Not so the legend under,
fixed, inexorable,
deep as the darkest mine
the thick rocks won't tell.

As fire burns the leaf
and out of the green appears
the vein in the center line
and the legend veins under there,

So, the world happens twice—
once what we see it as;
second it legends itself
deep, the way it is.

Outside

The least little sound sets the coyotes walking,
walking the edge of our comfortable earth.
We look inward, but all of them
are looking toward us as they walk the earth.

We need to let animals loose in our houses,
the wolf to escape with a pan in his teeth,
and streams of animals toward the horizon
racing with something silent in each mouth.

For all we have taken into our keeping
and polished with our hands belongs to a truth
greater than ours, in the animals' keeping.
Coyotes are circling around our truth.

Boom Town

Into any sound important
a snake puts out its tongue;
so at the edge of my home town
every snake listened.

And all night those oil well engines
went talking into the dark;
every beat fell through a snake,
quivering to the end.

This summer, home on a visit,
I walked out late one night;
only one hesitant pump, distant,
was remembering the past.

Often it faltered for breath
to prove how late it was;
the snakes, forgetting away through the grass,
had all closed their slim mouths.

Level Light

Sometimes the light when evening fails
stains all haystacked country and hills,
runs the cornrows and clasps the barn
with that kind of color escaped from corn
that brings to autumn the winter word—
a level shaft that tells the world:

> It is too late now for earlier ways;
> now there are only some other ways,
> and only one way to find them—fail.

In one stride night then takes the hill.

Two Evenings

I

Back of the stride of the power line
a dozen antelope dissolved into view,
but we in the car were fading away—
we were troubled about being ahead of time.

The world became like a slow mirror,
clear at first till images welled,
as if decisions could raise the sun
or eyes build faces in the quicksilver.

II

Today toward night when bats came out—
flyers so nervous they rest by turning
and foreknow collision by calling out "Maybe!"—
we anticipated something we did not expect.

Counting the secretaries coming out of a building
there were more people than purposes.
We stared at the sidewalk looking for ourselves,
like antelope fading into evening.

Ice-Fishing

Not thinking other than how the hand works
I wait until dark here on the cold
world rind, ice-curved over simplest rock,
where the tugged river flows over hidden
springs too insidious to be quite forgotten.

When the night comes I plunge my hand
where the string of fish know their share
of the minimum. Then, bringing back my hand
is a great sunburst event; and slow
home with me over unmarked snow

In the wild flipping warmth of won-back thought
my boots, my hat, my body go.

The Well Rising

The well rising without sound,
the spring on a hillside,
the plowshare brimming through deep ground
everywhere in the field—

The sharp swallows in their swerve
flaring and hesitating
hunting for the final curve
coming closer and closer—

The swallow heart from wing beat to wing beat
counseling decision, decision:
thunderous examples. I place my feet
with care in such a world.

A Ritual to Read to Each Other

If you don't know the kind of person I am
and I don't know the kind of person you are
a pattern that others made may prevail in the world
and following the wrong god home we may miss our star.

For there is many a small betrayal in the mind,
a shrug that lets the fragile sequence break
sending with shouts the horrible errors of childhood
storming out to play through the broken dyke.

And as elephants parade holding each elephant's tail,
but if one wanders the circus won't find the park,
I call it cruel and maybe the root of all cruelty
to know what occurs but not recognize the fact.

And so I appeal to a voice, to something shadowy,
a remote important region in all who talk:
though we could fool each other, we should consider—
lest the parade of our mutual life get lost in the dark.

For it is important that awake people be awake,
or a breaking line may discourage them back to sleep;
the signals we give—yes or no, or maybe—
should be clear: the darkness around us is deep.

Connections

Ours is a low, curst, under-swamp land
the raccoon puts his hand in,
gazing through his mask for tendrils
that will hold it all together.

No touch can find that thread, it is too small.
Sometimes we think we learn its course—
through evidence no court allows
a sneeze may glimpse us Paradise.

But ways without a surface we can find
flash through the mask only by surprise—
a touch of mud, a raccoon smile.

And if we purify the pond, the lilies die.

Acquaintance

Because our world hardened
while a wind was blowing
mountains hold a grim expression
and all the birds are crying.

I search in such terrain,
face flint all the way,
alert for the unreal
or the real gone astray.

And you I greet, gargoyles—
untrue, assuming no truth,
never expecting my compass,
built from the first on grief.

On the Glass Ice

It was time. Arriving at Long Lake the storm
shook flakes on the glass ice, and the frozen fish
all lay there surprised by February.

I skated hard in the beginning storm
in order to meet every flake. Polished,
the way rich men can wait for progress, the lake waited.

It got a real winter blanket—the day
going and the white eye losing downward,
the sky deeper and deeper. No sound.

In deep snow I knew the fish were singing.
I skated and skated till the lake was drowned.

Sayings from the Northern Ice

It is people at the edge who say
things at the edge: winter is toward knowing.

> Sled runners before they meet have long talk apart.
> There is a pup in every litter the wolves will have.
> A knife that falls points at an enemy.
> Rocks in the wind know their place: down low.
> Over your shoulder is God; the dying deer sees Him.

At the mouth of the long sack we fall in forever
storms brighten the spikes of the stars.

> Wind that buried bear skulls north of here
> and beats moth wings for help outside the door
> is bringing bear skull wisdom, but do not ask the skull
> too large a question till summer.
> Something too dark was held in that strong bone.

Better to end with a lucky saying:

> Sled runners cannot decide to join or to part.
> When they decide, it is a bad day.

It Is the Time You Think

Deaf to process, alive only to ends,
such are the thinkers around me, the logical ones—
the way in the yesterday forest, startled alert, a doe
would look along a gun barrel at Daniel Boone,
becoming the fringed shirt with instant recognition.

Deaf too, I stand on the peninsula of fear
remembering in their silent cars the newest hunters,
not the ones who stood with shadow faces
or stepped among the oaks and left the field,
but sudden men in jets who hunt the world.

And I think of the cold places in the river—
springs so deep it is hard to think about,
they come so wide and still into what we know
But, thinking, I would be sudden with all cold springs,
before the blend, at once, wherever the issue.

I would sweep the watch face, narrowing angles,
catching at things left here that are ours.
There must be a trick, a little pause before
real things happen—a little trap to manage events,
some kind of edge against the expected act.

I am too local a creature to take the truth
unless and until by God it happens to me.

Sunset: Southwest

In front of the courthouse holding the adaptable flag
Jesus will be here the day the world ends
looking off there into the sky-bore
past Socorro over sunset lands.

There will be torque in all the little towns,
wind will beat upon the still
face of anyone, just anyone,
who will stand and turn the still

Face to full dial staring out there
and then the world will be all—
the face hearing only the world
bloom from the eyes, and fall.

Following

There dwelt in a cave, and winding I thought lower,
a rubber bear that overcame his shadow;
and because he was not anything but good
he served all sorts of pretzel purposes.

When I met plausible men who called me noble,
I fed them to the bear, and—bulge! rear!—
the shadow never caught up with his girth,
as those talkers never caught up with their worth.

And Bear and I often went wild and frivolous,
following a way that we could create, or claim,
but we had to deal sometimes with the serious
who think they find the way when the way finds them.

In their deliberate living all is planned,
but they forget to squeak sometimes when the wheel comes round;
Bear and I and other such simple fellows
just count on the wheel, and the wheel remembers the sound.

56

Postscript

You reading this page, this trial—
shall we portion out the fault?
You call with your eyes for fodder,
demand bright frosting on your bread,
want the secret handclasp of jokes,
the nudges of innuendo.

And we both like ranting, swearing,
maybe calling of names:
can we meet this side of anger
somewhere in the band of mild sorrow?—
though many of our tastes have vanished,
and we depend on spice?—

Not you, not I—but something—
pales out in this trying for too much
and has brought us, wrong, together.
It is long since we've been lonely
and my track looking for Crusoe
could make you look up, calling, "Friday!"

Traveling Through
the Dark
1962

I. In Medias Res

Traveling Through the Dark

Traveling through the dark I found a deer
dead on the edge of the Wilson River road.
It is usually best to roll them into the canyon:
that road is narrow; to swerve might make more dead.

By glow of the tail-light I stumbled back of the car
and stood by the heap, a doe, a recent killing;
she had stiffened already, almost cold.
I dragged her off; she was large in the belly.

My fingers touching her side brought me the reason—
her side was warm; her fawn lay there waiting,
alive, still, never to be born.
Beside that mountain road I hesitated.

The car aimed ahead its lowered parking lights;
under the hood purred the steady engine.
I stood in the glare of the warm exhaust turning red;
around our group I could hear the wilderness listen.

I thought hard for us all—my only swerving—,
then pushed her over the edge into the river.

In Medias Res

On Main one night when they sounded the chimes
my father was ahead in shadow, my son
behind coming into the streetlight, on each side
a brother and a sister; and overhead
the chimes went arching for the perfect sound.
There was a one-stride god on Main that night,
all walkers in a cloud.

I saw pictures, windows taking shoppers
where the city went, a great shield hammering out,
my wife loving the stations on that shield
and following into the shades calling back.
I had not thought to know the hero quite so well.
"Aeneas!" I cried, "just man, defender!"
And our town burned and burned.

Elegy

The responsible sound of the lawnmower
puts a net under the afternoon;
closing the refrigerator door
I hear a voice in the other room
that starts up color in every cell:
        Presents like this, Father, I got from you,
        and there are hundreds more to tell.

One night, sound held in cornfield farms
drowned in August, and melonflower breath
creeping in stealth—we walked west
where all the rest of the country slept.
I hold that memory in both my arms—
        how the families there had starved the dogs;
        in the night they waited to be fed.

At the edge of dark there paled a flash—
a train came on with its soft tread
that roused itself with light and thundered
with dragged windows curving down earth's side
while the cornstalks whispered.
        All of us hungry creatures watched
        until it was extinguished.

If only once in all those years
the right goodby could have been said!
I hear you climbing up the snow,
a brown-clad wanderer on the road
with the usual crooked stick,
     and on the wrong side of the mountains
     I can hear the latches click.

Remember in the Southwest going down the canyons?
We turned off the engine, the tires went hoarse
picking up sound out of turned away mountains;
we felt the secret sky lean down.
Suddenly the car came to with a roar.
     And remember the Christmas wreath on our door—
     when we threw it away and it jumped blue up the fire?

At sight of angels or anything unusual
you are to mark the spot with a cross,
for I have set out to follow you
and these marked places are expected,
but in between I can hear no sound.
     The softest hush of doors I close
     may jump to slam in a March wind.

When you left our house that night and went falling
into that ocean, a message came: silence.
I pictured you going, spangles and bubbles
leaving your pockets in a wheel clockwise.
Sometimes I look out of our door at night.
     When you send messages they come spinning
     back into sound with just leaves rustling.

Come battering. I listen, am the same, waiting.

A Stared Story

Over the hill came horsemen, horsemen whistling.
They were all hard-driven, stamp, stamp, stamp.
Legs withdrawn and delivered again like pistons,
down they rode into the winter camp,
and while earth whirled on its forgotten center
those travelers feasted till dark in the lodge of their chief.
Into the night at last on earth their mother
they drummed away; the farthest hoofbeat ceased.

Often at cutbanks where roots hold dirt together
survivors pause in the sunlight, quiet, pretending
that stared story—and gazing at earth their mother:
all journey far, hearts beating, to some such ending.
And all, slung here in our cynical constellation,
whistle the wild world, live by imagination.

Thinking for Berky

In the late night listening from bed
I have joined the ambulance or the patrol
screaming toward some drama, the kind of end
that Berky must have some day, if she isn't dead.

The wildest of all, her father and mother cruel,
farming out there beyond the old stone quarry
where highschool lovers parked their lurching cars,
Berky learned to love in that dark school.

Early her face was turned away from home
toward any hardworking place; but still her soul,
with terrible things to do, was alive, looking out
for the rescue that—surely, some day——would have to come.

Windiest nights, Berky, I have thought for you,
and no matter how lucky I've been I've touched wood.
There are things not solved in our town though tomorrow came:
there are things time passing can never make come true.

We live in an occupied country, misunderstood;
justice will take us millions of intricate moves.
Sirens will hunt down Berky, you survivors in your beds
listening through the night, so far and good.

With My Crowbar Key

I do tricks in order to know:
careless I dance,
then turn to see
the mark to turn God left for me.

Making my home in vertigo
I pray with my screams
and think with my hair
prehensile in the dark with fear.

When I hear the well bucket strike something soft
far down at noon,
then there's no place
far enough away to hide my face.

When I see my town over sights of a rifle,
and carved by light
from the lowering sun,
then my old friends darken one by one.

By step and step like a cat toward God
I dedicated walk,
but under the house
I realize the kitten's crouch.

And by night like this I turn and come
to this possible house
which I open, and see
myself at work with this crowbar key.

Mouse Night: One of Our Games

We heard thunder. Nothing great—on high
ground rain began. Who ran through
that rain? I shrank, a fieldmouse, when
the thunder came—under grass with bombs
of water scything stems. My tremendous
father cowered: "Lions rushing make
that sound," he said; "we'll be brain-washed
for sure if head-size chunks of water hit us.
Duck and cover! It takes a man
to be a mouse this night," he said.

The Thought Machine

Its little eye stares "On" in its forehead
by its maker's name. They say it anticipates
its memories and holds "Eureka!" tight
in little wheels so sure that all steel
hardens when incorporated in it.
The only Please it knows is, Be Correct;
but it can tolerate mistakes.

You tell your troubles to it, how your letters
all came back with no acknowledgment
and all you wanted was assurance all was known.
It tugs its collar; its little eye glows on.
You tell about the woman at the corner
ringing the bell to bring Jesus and his weather.
That is long ago.

You tell of the hill that never attracted the deer;
you think it frightened them, a fear place,
where you always had to go to listen—it was
for your town and for the world; it was for . . .—
and you are back there, listening again:
the little eye goes kind; the forehead
has the noble look that hill had.

66

And the world whirls into vision; in Tibet
a prayer wheel turns for you; an Eskimo
by such a northern fire lives that you live so,
touching only important things;
you see that all machines belong;
the deer are safe;
a letter has reached home.

Parentage

My father didn't really belong in history.
He kept looking over his shoulder at some mistake.
He was a stranger to me, for I belong.

There never was a particular he couldn't understand,
but there were too many in too long a row,
and like many another he was overwhelmed.

Today drinking coffee I look over the cup
and want to have the right amount of fear,
preferring to be saved and not, like him, heroic.

I want to be as afraid as the teeth are big,
I want to be as dumb as the wise are wrong:
I'd just as soon be pushed by events to where I belong.

The Research Team in the Mountains

We have found a certain heavy kind of wolf.
Haven't seen it, though—
just *know* it.

Answers are just echoes, they say. But
a question travels before it comes back,
and that counts.

Did you know that here everything is free?
We've found days that wouldn't allow a price
on anything.

When a dirty river and a clean river
come together the result is—
dirty river.

If your policy is to be friends in the mountains
a rock falls on you: the only real friends—
you can't help it.

Many go home having "conquered a mountain"—
they leave their names at the top in a jar
for snow to remember.

Looking out over the campfire at night
again this year I pick a storm for you,
again the first one.

We climbed Lostine and Hurricane and Chief Joseph canyons;
finally in every canyon the road ends.
Above that—storms of stone.

Holding the Sky

We saw a town by the track in Colorado.
Cedar trees below had sifted the air,
snow water foamed the torn river there,
and a lost road went climbing the slope like a ladder.

We were traveling between a mountain and Thursday,
holding pages back on the calendar,
remembering every turn in the roadway:
we could hold that sky, we said, and remember.

On the western slope we crashed into Thursday.
"So long," you said when the train stopped there.
Snow was falling, touching in the air.
Those dark mountains have never wavered.

The Job

It starts before light—
all that story of the stars,
night winking meaning,
dawn still frozen, and in dark spells
in our little town, at zero in winter,
from every house plumed furnaces announcing themselves;
from our house a great gray promise
promising upward and out from town: dawn.

We feel confident.
Into some local brain we think the story will come
like swallows into a house, anyone's head, any thought's home.
The church rises from its trees and holds
its true darkness tall, nearly visible,
then really tall till the earth rings; the bells
only swing in the cold silently opening
their mouths; and we walk into the call of the college.

Now the hall takes us toward quiet,
past the stairwell where Foucault's pendulum
remembers how the earth used to spin;
we turn again, enter the classroom,
look at the deep faces looking at us,
deep in our school, waiting under the school roof;
we open the book with care and hold our breath:
begin—translating the vast versions of the wind.

Prairie Town

There was a river under First and Main;
the salt mines honeycombed farther down.
A wealth of sun and wind ever so strong
converged on that home town, long gone.

At the north edge there were the sandhills.
I used to stare for hours at prairie dogs,
which had their town, and folded their little paws
to stare beyond their fence where I was.

River rolling in secret, salt mines with care
holding your crystals and stillness, north prairie—
what kind of trip can I make, with what old friend,
ever to find a town so widely rich again?

Pioneers, for whom history was walking through dead grass,
and the main things that happened were miles and the time of day—
you built that town, and I have let it pass.
Little folded paws, judge me: I came away.

Conservative

Indiana felt the ice,
yet holds wide lakes against that pain:
I lived in Indiana once,
put these hands into those lakes
of counties near Fort Wayne.

You come a river, then our town
where summer domes the elms that hide
the river, which—a lurking home—
reflects in windows all the clouds
that drift that countryside.

All you that live your city way:
you cannot hold thought ways to hold
the old way steady; nowadays
you cannot hear the songs we sang
or know what glaciers told,

So I'll say this, then stand apart,
allegiant to where we lived
all the way to cross my heart:
Your years—these riffles atoms made—
and your map river-carved

Conceal a map new glaciers plan,
and there are rivers yet to come,
wide lakes again, and maybe hands
to dip like mine, a voice to say:
"For towns, I'll take this one."

Tornado

First the soul of our house left, up the chimney,
and part of the front window went outward—pursued
whatever tore at the chest. Part of the lake
on top guyed around the point, bellied
like a tent; and fish like seeds ripened felt
a noiseless Command around their gills, while
the wheatfields crouched, reminded with a hand.

That treble talk always at the bottom of the creek
at the mouth, where the lake leaned away from the rock
at the mouth, rose above water. Then Command moved
away again and our town spread, ruined
but relieved, at the bottom of its remembered air.
We weren't left religion exactly (the church
was ecumenical bricks), but a certain tall element:
a pulse beat still in the stilled rock
and in the buried sound along the buried mouth of the creek.

The Old Hamer Place

The wind came every night like an animal
rushing our house, disappearing before day,
leaving us all we could stand of the way it would be
when a hand always raised over the world fell,
or when horizontal tomorrow dimensioned out
from a scene so deep it captured our eyes.
    The animal made off thrashing limbs,
    taking a message in its heavy shoulders
    into the lean hills among the low stars, crashing.

All this had got lost from my mind: now
no one in all the world tonight is
even thinking about that hollow house
when the truck left years ago and the moaning
seasons began to wander through the room, stirring
vines and their shadows that grew in the dark.
    I touch that wall, collapsing it there where
    no one knows, by the quavering owl sound
    in a forest no one knows.

But the world is loaded with places for tomorrow to visit,
though this had got lost from my mind,
how the truck left years ago.
Enough air moves any morning for stillness to
come where the windows are. A place that
changed is a different place, but
    A whole town might come shuddering back, that had disappeared
    when a dark animal began to overcome the world
    and a litle bird came to sing our walls down.

The Woman at Banff

While she was talking a bear happened along, violating
every garbage can. Shaking its loose, Churchillian,
V for victory suit, it ripped up and ate
a greasy "Bears Are Dangerous!" sign.

While she was talking the trees above signalled—
"Few," and the rock back of them—"Cold."
And while she was talking a moose—huge, black—
swam that river and faded off winterward,

Up toward the Saskatchewan.

The Tillamook Burn

These mountains have heard God;
they burned for weeks. He spoke
in a tongue of flame from sawmill trash
and you can read His word down to the rock.

In milky rivers the steelhead
butt upstream to spawn
and find a world with depth again,
starting from stillness and water across gray stone.

Inland along the canyons
all night weather smokes
past the deer and the widow-makers—
trees too dead to fall till again He speaks,

Mowing the criss-cross trees and the listening peaks.

On Quitting a Little College

By footworn boards, by steps
that sagged years after the pride of workmen,
by things that had to *do* so long they now seemed right,
by ways of acting so old they grooved the people
(and all this among fields that never quit
under a patient sky),
I taught. And then I quit.

"Let's walk home," the president said.
He faced down the street,
and on the rollers of bird flight
through the year-round air
that little town became all it had promised him.
He could not quit; he could not let go fast enough;
his duties carried him.

The bitter habit of the forlorn cause
is my addiction. I miss it now, but face
ahead and go in my own way
toward my own place.

Reporting Back

By the secret that holds the forest up,
no one will escape. (We have reached this place.)

The sky will come home some day.
(We pay all mistakes our bodies make when they move.)

Is there a way to walk that living has obscured?
(Our feet are trying to remember some path we are walking toward.)

The Poets' Annual Indigence Report

Tonight beyond the determined moon,
aloft with nothing left that is voluntary
for delight, everything uttering hydrogen,
your thinkers are mincing along through a hail of contingencies,

While we all—floating though we are, lonesome though we are,
lost in hydrogen—we live by seems things:
when things just *are*, then something else
will be doing the living.

Doing is not enough; being is not enough;
knowing is far from enough. So we clump around, putting
feet on the dazzle floor, awaiting the real schedule
by celebrating the dazzle schedule.

And, whatever is happening, we are here;
a lurch or a god has brought us together.
We do our jobs—listening in fear
in endless, friendless, Jesus-may-happen fashion.

Our shadows ride over the grass, your shadows, ours:—
Rich men, wise men, be our contemporaries.

In Response to a Question

The earth says have a place, be what that place
requires; hear the sound the birds imply
and see as deep as ridges go behind
each other. (Some people call their scenery flat,
their only picture framed by what they know:
I think around them rise a riches and a loss
too equal for their chart—but absolutely tall.)

The earth says every summer have a ranch
that's minimum: one tree, one well, a landscape
that proclaims a universe—sermon
of the hills, hallelujah mountain,
highway guided by the way the world is tilted,
reduplication of mirage, flat evening:
a kind of ritual for the wavering.

75

The earth says where you live wear the kind
of color that your life is (gray shirt for me)
and by listening with the same bowed head that sings
draw all into one song, join
the sparrow on the lawn, and row that easy
way, the rage without met by the wings
within that guide you anywhere the wind blows.

Listening, I think that's what the earth says.

With One Launched Look

The cheetah levels at one far deer
rejecting all others in his charge,
connecting toward the chosen throat
—a dedicated follower.

It is that choice that quells the deer,
such a fateful diagram:
bisecting all the irrelevant world
—one launched look and its afterward.

B.C.

The seed that met water spoke a little name.

(Great sunflowers were lording the air that day;
this was before Jesus, before Rome; that other air
was readying our hundreds of years to say things
that rain has beat down on over broken stones
and heaped behind us in many slag lands.)

Quiet in the earth a drop of water came,
and the little seed spoke: "Sequoia is my name."

Captive

Calmly through the bars observe
how correct a tiger is:
the striped fur blends with cages;
how the iron parallels
the paw freed by your—calmly!—eye;
and if it's a big one—coincide—
how the stripes become the bars:
tiger flesh rejoins a fawn's,
commitment to the cub he was
before a shadow caged his ribs;
how he glides by appropriateness
into jungles while you stand
outside his eyes, beyond his bars:
captor, witness, victim—calmed.

The View from Here

In Antarctica drooping their little shoulders
like bottles the penguins stand, small,
sad, black—and the wind
bites hard over them.

Edging that continent they huddle to turn their eyes.
Penguins, we can't help you; and all that cold
hangs over us too, wide beyond thought.
We too stand and wait.

Lit Instructor

Day after day up there beating my wings
with all of the softness truth requires
I feel them shrug whenever I pause:
they class my voice among tentative things,

And they credit fact, force, battering.
I dance my way toward the family of knowing,
embracing stray error as a long-lost boy
and bringing him home with my fluttering.

Every quick feather asserts asserts a just claim;
it bites like a saw into white pine.
I communicate right; but explain to the dean—
well, Right has a long and intricate name.

And the saying of it is a lonely thing.

The Star in the Hills

A star hit in the hills behind our house
up where the grass turns brown touching the sky.

Meteors have hit the world before, but this was near,
and since TV; few saw, but many felt the shock.
The state of California owns that land
(and out from shore three miles), and any stars
that come will be roped off and viewed on week days 8 to 5.

A guard who took the oath of loyalty and denied
any police record told me this:
"If you don't have a police record yet
you could take the oath and get a job
if California should be hit by another star."

"I'd promise to be loyal to California
and to guard any stars that hit it," I said,
"or any place three miles out from shore,
unless the star was bigger than the state—
in which case I'd be loyal to *it*."

But he said no exceptions were allowed,
and he leaned against the state-owned meteor
so calm and puffed a cork-tip cigarette
that I looked down and traced with my foot in the dust
and thought again and said, "OK—any star."

I Was in the City All Day

Into the desert, trading people for horses,
the leader rode toward a responsible act:
the having one person at the last campfire,
telling just the next thing to that one person,
with all around only the waiting night waiting,
in the shadows horses eating wild hay—
and then the last word without distraction,
one meaning like a bird slipping out into the dark.

A Poet to a Novelist

When we write, fighting feedback, eedback, dback,
back, ack of the forward part of our brains,
a perfect flower blooms from all failure; we hear
every wrong number down a tincan telephone line jangle the bells
till the neighbors' ears are supporting the line,
everybody's effort scaled down, aled down, d down, down
toward disappearing—all who lunge plunging.
We let them go by at the world's pace.

There are hills our windows give every winter;
when we close the curtain we know the streetlight is left
outside alone; from the end of the street (this is the edge of town)
the few slant flakes come out of the dark and fall on the house
that goes deaf while night fans over the roof.

Such arrivals in storms are one kind of chance,
a difference we want after our days doing
one thing at a time, the way purpose is.

We take everything stacked, being all at once
like a jewel and then into some act; we pass calendar knots
through our hands, remembering not just important things—
maybe the welcome a Western town gave early women,
dust from the alley past the clothesline, anybody's sky
sighting down given streets, years like a fan opening
and then closing. We pay it out (still owing what's near us
every aid, no matter the worth, because it is near).

We hear such blossom syllables in the sounds that rise
that we cannot find a path among true words,
redundant honesty of the scrupulous; we go down
with what occurs to any length, echoes realer
than originals, coming from cliffs the air belongs on
or comes back to sideways. We happen in the night
on orchards that stutter whiteness as the moon passes:
spring comes every night when luck is there.

We owe the twilight aid because day
once prevailed: the bad parts run a world
ready to fade but still present if a person
will come out from his eyes and be willing to hold
what he views. We welcome all back the child's way—
the finding of new things or sorting through gravel
or discovering the scent of alfalfa
that knows water out of the desert in the evening.

Over the night arc our need reaches for duty,
our state a glimmer to be good. Putting down
the last book or finding the light on the wall
by feel and memory, we veer toward the saintly,
say "Sorry!" (But we rebel at only the good:—
read and do what you want, and don't even be eager
to find the best—no finicky appetites.) No place
is wide enough to be sorry in, not any place.

Because you walk for us, we call you this,
"pilgrim for rain." No one else will meet us
low enough to hear wind in the grass
and let it go over our place. We wait,
low and looking for the oat spire against the sun,
leaf and straw, hay attached by accident to the ground.
Because we write we know the cost
of every day—the cost is all the rest.

Because you know it so, I give you this.

Universe Is One Place

Crisis they call it?—when
when the gentle wheat leans at the combine and
and the farm girl brings cool jugs wrapped in burlap
slapping at her legs?

We think—drinking cold water
water looking at the sky—
Sky is home, universe is one place.
Crisis? City folks make

Make such a stir.
Farm girl away through the wheat.

In the Night Desert

The Apache word for love twists
    then numbs the tongue:
Uttered once clear, said—
    never that word again.

"Cousin," you call, or "Sister" and one
    more word that spins
In the dust: a talk-flake
    chipped like obsidian.

The girl who hears this flake and
    follows you into the dark
Turns at a touch: the night desert
    forever behind her back.

II. Before the Big Storm

Before the Big Storm

You are famous in my mind.
When anyone mentions your name
all the boxes marked "1930's"
fall off the shelves;
and the orators on the Fourth of July
all begin shouting again.
The audience of our high school commencement
begin to look out of the windows at the big storm.

And I think of you in our play—
oh, helpless and lonely!—crying,
and your father is dead again.
He was drunk; he fell.

When they mention your name,
our houses out there in the wind
creak again in the storm;
and I lean from our play, wherever I am,
to you, quiet at the edge of that town:
"All the world is blowing away."
"It is almost daylight."
"Are you warm?"

Things We Did That Meant Something

Thin as memory to a bloodhound's nose,
being the edge of some new knowing,
I often glance at a winter color—
husk or stalk, a sunlight touch,
maybe a wasp nest in the brush
near the winter river with silt like silver.

Once with a slingshot I hit a wasp nest:—
without direction but sure of right,
released from belief and into act,
hornets planed off by their sincere faith.
Vehement response for them was enough,
patrolling my head with its thought like a moth:—

"Sometime the world may be hit like this
or I getting lost may walk toward this color
far in old sunlight with no trace at all,
till only the grass will know I fall."

At Liberty School

Girl in the front row who had no mother
and went home evey day to get supper,
the class became silent when you left early.

Elaborate histories were in our book
but of all the races you were the good:
the taxes of Rome were at your feet.

When the bell rang we did not write any more.
Traitor to everything else, we poured
to the fountain. I bent and thought of you.

Our town now is Atlantis, crystal-water-bound;
at the door of the schoolhouse fish are swimming round;
thinking in and out of the church tower go deep waves.

Girl in the front row who had no mother,
as I passed the alleys of our town toward supper
there were not spiteful nails in any board.

Lake Chelan

They call it regional, this relevance—
the deepest place we have: in this pool forms
the model of our land, a lonely one,
responsive to the wind. Everything we own
has brought us here: from here we speak.

The sun stalks among these peaks to sight
the lake down aisles, long like a gun;
a ferryboat, lost by a century, toots
for trappers, the pelt of the mountains
rinsed in the sun and that sound.

Suppose a person far off to whom this lake
occurs: told a problem, he might hear a word
so dark he drowns an instant, and stands dumb
for the centuries of his country and the suave
hills beyond the stranger's sight.

Is this man dumb, then, for whom Chelan lives
in the wilderness? On the street you've seen
someone like a trapper's child pause,
and fill his eyes with some irrelevant flood—
a tide stops him, delayed in his job.

Permissive as a beach, he turns inland,
harks like a fire, glances through the dark
like an animal drinking, and arrives along that line
a lake has found far back in the hills
where what comes finds a brim gravity exactly requires.

Summer Will Rise

Summer will rise till the houses fear;
streets will hear underground streams;
purple, the banished color, will flare.
This is the town where the vine will come.

People will listen but will not hear.
Eyes will wizen to find a friend.
When no one is watching the candleflame
this is the town where the wind will come.

The trees will hear, farther than winter,
over the town a coming of birds.
What great wild hands will reach for them?
—and for all who are here when those wanderers come?

Fall Journey

Evening came, a paw, to the gray hut by the river.
Pushing the door with a stick, I opened it.
Only a long walk had brought me there,
steps into the continent they had placed before me.

I read weathered log, stone fireplace, broken chair,
the dead grass outside under the cottonwood tree—
and it all stared back. We've met before, my memory
started to say, somewhere. . . .

And then I stopped: my father's eyes were gray.

Late at Night

Falling separate into the dark
the hailstone yelps of geese pattered
through our roof; startled we listened.

Those V's of direction swept by unseen
so orderly that we paused. But then
faltering back through their circle they came.

Were they lost up there in the night?
They always knew the way, we thought.
You looked at me across the room:—

We live in a terrible season.

The Museum at Tillamook

Still faces on the wall: that look
the early camera gave—hold still for time.
We walk down the corridor, looking history
back and forth: spearheads in one room,
bombs and pictures of our Navy blimp
in another, one hundred years between.

Joe Champion: first white settler,
hater of statistics, non-average.
(Indian Adams gave relics for the story.)
Joe carved this thing to eat with—a spoon,
sort of; he made this cradle for a baby
and this other kind of cradle, for grain.

Here is the hollow tree Joe inhabited—
his house, at first, before he taught
and prospered and died.
(Sold 500 acres for $400—got rich that way.)
Where's his grave?

This dugout—canoe or coffin—came down the flood
in 1949, buried six feet deep in the Nehalem Spit.
There's "The Morning Star," all sails spread,
near the twins, age 84.
One of them—older looking—saw something
above the camera: the eyes go back. . . .

Upstairs other creatures from the wild
have gathered—cold, natural scenes: an owl of snow,
a wolf with clear eyes looking down over the blown
birds' eggs, through the floor
past The Morning Star
into Joe's hollow tree.

A Dedication

We stood by the library. It was an August night.
Priests and sisters of hundreds of unsaid creeds
passed us going their separate pondered roads.
We watched them cross under the corner light.

Freights on the edge of town were carrying away
flatcars of steel to be made into secret guns;
we knew, being human, that they were enemy guns,
and we were somehow vowed to poverty.

No one stopped or looked long or held out a hand.
They were following orders received from hour to hour,
so many signals, all strange, from a foreign power:
But tomorrow, you whispered, *peace may flow over the land.*

At that corner in a flash of lightning we two stood;
that glimpse we had will stare through the dark forever:
on the poorest roads we would be walkers and beggars,
toward some deathless meeting involving a crust of bread.

Chickens the Weasel Killed

A passerby being fair about sacrifice,
with no program but walking,
no acrobat of salvation,
I couldn't help seeing the weasel
fasten on the throat.

Any vision isolates:
those chickens the weasel killed—
I hear them relax years from now,
subsiding while they threaten,
and then appeal to the ground with their wings.

Requiem

Mother is gone. Bird songs wouldn't let her breathe.
The skating bug broke through the eternal veil.
A tree in the forest fell; the air remembered.
Two rocks clinked in the night to signal some meaning.

Traveler north, beyond where you can return,
hearing above you the last of the razor birds whizz
over the drift of dust that bore your name,
there's a kind of waiting you teach us—the art of not knowing.

Suicidal gestures of nobility driven to the wrist,
our molten bodies remembering some easier form,
we feel the bones assert the rites of yesterday
and the flow of angular events becoming destiny.

Summer and locusts own the elm part of town;
on the millpond moss is making its cream.
Our duty is just a certain high kind of waiting;
beyond our hearing is the hearing of the community.

The Last Friend

In every life poor body earns its own evil,
some promised blow or sickness that will be final;
hungrily searching, poor body gets killed.

A long romance curves down toward that marriage—
a radiant virus, a processional fever.
Hear the peals of reunion in the broken-hearted aged!

Somewhere in a hall, hear the bride hurry
toward a meeting of rapture to which all are bidden—
poor body, poor lover, in one grave buried.

"The Lyf So Short . . ."

We have lived in that room larger than the world,
cage in gold, corona in the dark,
where Chaucer let the pen go its quiet work
netting Criseyde, weeping as he wrote.

That man in the monk's hood climbs through flower stems
looking up at us his condemned man's look:
on secret pilings an imagined tide goes out,
over the sky go padding feet,

While we are forced backward into our dreams.
We are all sons of medieval kings;
"O alma redemptoris" is a grain on our tongue,
but no saint's hand can pluck the pain from us:—

Today we have to stand in absolute rain
and face whatever comes from God,
or stoop to smooth the earth over little things
that went into dirt, out of the world.

The Only Card I Got on My Birthday
Was from an Insurance Man

On upland farms into abandoned wells
on a line meridian high
state by state my birthday star comes on
and peers, my birthday night,
and in my eyes it stands while past its light
the world and I turn, just and far, till
every well scans over the year like spokes
of a wheel returning the long soft look of the sky.

Star in a well, dark message: when I die,
my glance drawn over galaxies,
all through one night let a candle nurse the dark
to mark this instant of what I was,
this once—not putting my hand out
blessing for business' sake any frail markers
of human years: we want real friends or none;
what's genuine will accompany every man.

Who travel these lonely wells can drink that star.

At the Old Place

The beak of dawn's rooster pecked
in the sky, and early Ella
called us.
I awoke to worse than sleep,
saw things clear beyond the barn,
and Ella older.

That was years—barns—ago.
But should another rooster crow
I'd be more wise,
listen better in the dawn,
wake at once to more than day—
to Ella always.

Love the Butcher Bird Lurks Everywhere

A gather of apricots fruit pickers left
gleam like reasons for light going higher, higher;
I look half as hard as I can to tease
the fruit out of its green.
    (It is time to run lest pity overtake us,
      and calamity pity invents to accompany itself:
      to sigh is a stern act—we are judged by this air.)

Down the steady eye of the charging bear
a gun barrel swerves—intention, then flame;
and willows do tricks to find an exact place in the wind:
resolution steady, bent to be true.
    (While there's time
    I call to you by all these dubious guides:
    "Forsake all ways except the way we came.")

Learning

A needle knows everything lengthwise
enforcing only the least radius
being hardly meant at all,
single, straight, serious.
    But it is late, it is always late.

If I knew enough it would all be gradual,
every departure, every arrival,
small radius, in, out, returning,
like the needle's eye always learning.
    But it is late, it is always late.

Worlds can swerve while I stammer;
the stars come different at night and nearer.
I can't learn even how to enter
what awaits me every year.

    And it is late, I know it.

In the Museum

Like that, I put the next thing in your hand—
this piece of rock the farthest climbers found,
or this, a broken urn volcano-finished.

Later you'll walk out and say, "Where's home?"
There will be something lacking in each room,
a part you held and casually laid down.

You never can get back, but there'll be other
talismans. You have learned to falter
in this good way: stand still, walk on, remember—

Let one by one things come alive like fish
and swim away into their future waves.

Time's Exile

From all encounters vintages ensue,
bitter, flat, or redolent. When we met
sunflowers were in bloom.
They mark the highway into Kansas yet.

My unreal errands, once the sun goes down,
fade into streetlight shadows.
Extenuate as the bright lights will, they run
into the hometown shadows.

I'm alongside old happenings when they flare;
like the dog that found the wounded quail
that came up through breast-feather shadows
into the sights and set their wings and sailed

The proximate field, and melted with shot
into another field—I bring things back from everywhere.
I am a man who detours through the park,
a man like those we used to meet back there—

Whose father had a son,
who has a son,
who finds his way by sunflowers through the dark.

Adults Only

Animals own a fur world;
people own worlds that are variously, pleasingly, bare.
And the way these worlds *are* once arrived for us kids
    with a jolt,
that night when the wild woman danced
in the giant cage we found we were all in
at the state fair.

Better women exist, no doubt, than that one,
and occasions more edifying, too, I suppose.
But we have to witness for ourselves what comes for us,
nor be distracted by barkers of irrelevant ware;
and a pretty good world, I say, arrived that night
when that woman came farming right out of her clothes,
by God,

At the state fair.

Wisteria Jones

She used to write, ribboning our talk away,
turning it onto itself many layers
and steeping the prose hills into purple highlands,
merely by distancing.

"Purple is the realest thing about the hills,"
she used to say—
"it's where we used to stand."
If I met her today I'd say that now.

Birthday

We have a dog named "Here";
the tame half wags; the bitter
half will freeze, paw still,
and look at the place the world came from.
I have explored Here's shoulder,
patting it. There is a muscle there
that levels mountains, or forbids.

The weather is telling Here a north story:
someone is lost in a waver of peaks in snow,
and only he gets the signal, tired;
has to turn north, even to teeth of the wind—
that is the only road to go,
through storm dark, by seams in the rock, peering.
Someone is always calling out in the snow.

Here stands by me. I am forty-five,
deep in a story strongly told. I've turned;
I know I will again—a straightness
never quite attained. The curve I try
to find becomes a late intention.
I pat Here's shoulder sometimes,
and we watch the clear sky bend.

Glances

Two people meet. The sky turns winter,
quells whatever they would say.
Then, a periphery glance into danger—
and an avalanche already on its way.

They have been honest all of their lives;
careful, calm, never in haste;
they didn't know what it is to *meet*.
Now they have met: the world is waste.

They find they are riding an avalanche
feeling at rest, all danger gone.
The present looks out of their eyes; they stand
calm and still on a speeding stone.

Fall Wind

Pods of summer crowd around the door;
I take them in the autumn of my hands.

Last night I heard the first cold wind outside;
the wind blew soft, and yet I shiver twice:

Once for thin walls, once for the sound of time.

A Pippa Lilted

Good things will happen
when the green flame of spring
goes up into hills where
we'd have our ranch if
we had the money.

It will be soon—
we'll hold our arms ready,
long toward the table
like Cézanne's people,
and let the light pour.

Just wait a little more—
let new errors cancel
the things we did wrong.
That's the right way for us:
our errors will dance.

It will be soon;
good things will happen.

The Trip

Our car was fierce enough;
no one could tell we were only ourselves;
so we drove, equals of the car,
and ate at a drive-in where Citizens were dining.
A waitress with eyes made up to be Eyes
brought food spiced by the neon light.

Watching, we saw the manager greet people—
hollow on the outside, some kind of solid veneer.
When we got back on the road we welcomed
it as a fierce thing welcomes the cold.
Some people you meet are so dull
that you always remember their names.

III. Representing Far Places

Representing Far Places

In the canoe wilderness branches wait for winter;
every leaf concentrates; a drop from the paddle falls.
Up through water at the dip of a falling leaf
to the sky's drop of light or the smell of another star
fish in the lake leap arcs of realization,
hard fins prying out from the dark below.

Often in society when the talk turns witty
you think of that place, and can't polarize at all:
it would be a kind of treason. The land fans in your head
canyon by canyon; steep roads diverge.
Representing far places you stand in the room,
all that you know merely a weight in the weather.

96

It is all right to be simply the way you have to be,
among contradictory ridges in some crescendo of knowing.

Long Distance

Sometimes when you watch the fire
ashes glow and gray
the way the sun turned cold on spires
in winter in the town back home
so far away.

Sometimes on the telephone
the one you hear goes far
and ghostly voices whisper in.
You think they are from other wires.
You think they are.

The Peters Family

At the end of their ragged field
a new field began:
miles told the sunset that Kansas
would hardly ever end,
and that beyond the Cimarron crossing
and after the row-crop land
a lake would surprise the country
and sag with a million birds.

You couldn't analyze those people—
a no-pattern had happened to them:
their field opened and opened,
level, and more, then forever,
never crossed. Their world went everywhere.

97

From the Gradual Grass

Imagine a voice calling,
"There is a voice now calling,"
or maybe a blasting cry:
"Walls are falling!"
as it makes walls be falling.

Then from the gradual grass,
too serious to be only noise—
whatever it is grass makes,
making words, a voice:
"Destruction is ending; this voice

"Is promising quiet: silence
by lasting forever grows to sound
endlessly from the world's end
promising, calling."
Imagine. *That voice is calling.*

In Fear and Valor

My mother was afraid
and in my life her fear has hid:
when Perseus holds the Gorgon's head,
she cringes, naked.

Clothed in my body, wild,
even as I grew strong,
my mother, weeping, suffered
the whole world's wrong.

Vanquished and trembling before she died,
she claimed a place in my every limb:
my mother, lost in my stride, fears Death,
as I hunt him.

The Title Comes Later

In my sleep a little man cries, "Faker! Faker!"
and I tell myself mildly and seriously
    that it is well to listen;
but in sleep it is that I evade: awake,
I meet the whole weather of my life,
    cold and real.
(The title is "Remembering, or
Guide Your Dreams Awake.")

In sleep all dreams belong, correcting each other;
but in blizzards of our waking all possible worlds
    are fighting each other.
"Every act in every dream deserves to live,"
I tell myself, mildly and seriously:
    "accept the law that grounds your being;
awake, asleep, or neither, everything belongs."
But awaking from awaking, I am a little man myself crying,
    "Faker! Faker!"

At Cove on the Crooked River

At Cove at our camp in the open canyon
it was the kind of place where you might look out
some evening and see trouble walking away.

And the river there meant something
always coming from snow and flashing around boulders
after shadow-fish lurking below the mesa.

We stood with wet towels over our heads for shade,
looking past the Indian picture rock and the kind of trees
that act out whatever has happened to them.

Oh civilization, I want to carve you like this,
decisively outward the way evening comes
over that kind of twist in the scenery

When people cramp into their station wagons
and roll up the windows, and drive away.

Last Vacation

Mountains crowded around on the north.
Hoisting our cage we went walk, walk.
Where, however, was home?
Tired, we set our cage down.

A zebra view. The black we could see through,
past that other, past its fire;
we could look out far through the black.
But glowing between lay the bars world:

Like an old house where our hearts had beat,
like a window burning at the end of our street.
The calendar fell for thirty days
like a bent jail sky over two meteors.

Looking for Someone

1

Many a time driving over the Coast Range,
down the cool side—hemlock, spruce, then shore pine—
I've known something I should have said one time:
"If we hadn't met, then everything would have to change."

2

We were judged; our shadows knew our height,
and after dark, exact, the air confirmed
all with its move or stillness:
we both were trapped on an odd-shaped island.

3

Sleet persuades a traveler: I all night
know no under the earth escape
even when the sky goes back remote.
Walking till the stars forget, I look out

4

And watch the smoke at Astoria and Seaside
cringing along the coast, and barefoot gulls
designing the sand: "Go flat, go flat,"—the waves;
the little boat, the mild riding light,

5

The sand going democratic, trading places down the wind,
everything distancing away. Finding this
took all this time, and you're not even here.
Though we met, everything had to change.

What God Used for Eyes Before We Came

At night sometimes the big fog roams in tall
from the coast and away tall on the mountain road
it stands without moving while cars wander along
in the canyons they make with their lights maintaining the worth
of local things. Along the continent shelf and back
far for searching the light engages the stone.

The brain blurring to know wanders that road,
goes the way Jesus came, irresistible,
calm over irrelevant history
toward a continent wall that moth rays touch—
our land backed by being old at night, lying deep,
the gray air holding ruin rock at Hovenweep.

Found in a Storm

A storm that needed a mountain
met it where we were:
we woke up in a gale
that was reasoning with our tent,
and all the persuaded snow
streaked along, guessing the ground.

We turned from that curtain, down.
But sometime we will turn
back to the curtain and go
by plan through an unplanned storm,
disappearing into the cold,
meanings in search of a world.

Returned to Say

When I face north a lost Cree
on some new shore puts a moccasin down,
rock in the light and noon for seeing,
he in a hurry and I beside him.

It will be a long trip; he will be a new chief;
we have drunk new water from an unnamed stream;
under little dark trees he is to find a path
we both must travel because we have met.

102

Henceforth we gesture even by waiting;
there is a grain of sand on his knifeblade
so small he blows it and while his breathing
darkens the steel his eyes become set

And start a new vision: the rest of his life.
We will mean what he does. Back of this page
the path turns north. We are looking for a sign.
Our moccasins do not mark the ground.

A Look Returned

At the border of October
where Montana meets Alberta
that white grass that worshipped wind
climbed from summer to the sky,
which began to change.

I saw that day that day relate
winter's province to the state,
and clouds correct the fence's stance
where a hill twisted the line
of the seamless land.

All countries have their majesties
and meet October in various ways,
harking toward wonder every winter,
trying again for their best picture
at their best times;

But that state so north it curled behind
the map in hands of snow and wind,
clutching the end of no place—
I hold that state before my face,
and learn my life.

Late Thinker

Remembering mountain farms
that gleam far for lost men,
he knows by sympathy
tonight by the steady stove,
questioning one grain at a time,
wandering like a dune,
easy with the wind—
that some kind of organization
is the right way to live.

A secret friend of those lands
where certain plants hide in the woods,
he stands with them. In the fern
he shoulders pack. In the dark
he joins the star-striding men
who crossed the continent
following, toward the low sky,
ocean-generous clouds
to the firred mountains of Oregon

Or maybe—tie, rail, spike—
to hay towns beyond Salt Lake:
store fronts winds have tasted,
paint that summers tested—
he questions those pale towns,
turns to those haggard lands.
Where are the wrongs men have done?
He holds out calloused hands
toward that landscape of justice.

He counts each daily meeting,
the stare of its blind meaning,
and maintains an autumn allegiance,
but what can he lean toward?
Remembering the wild places, bitter,
where pale fields meet winter,
he searches for some right song
that could catch and then shake the world,
any night by the steady stove.

Interlude

Think of a river beyond your thought
avoiding your sight by being so pure
that it can turn anywhere any rocks says
but always be ready for the next real call,
and beyond such a river this ritual night
think of summer weather questioning the corn
contoured for rain, while the lightning crawls,
and a face like a news event approaches the world.

Then come back in our cave of space
and wait for the wonder of that face.

In Dear Detail, by Ideal Light

1

Night huddled our town,
plunged from the sky.
You moved away.
I save what I can of the time.

In other towns, calling my name,
home people hale me, dazed;
those moments we hold,
reciting in the evening,

Reciting about you, receding
through the huddle of any new town.
Can we rescue the light
that happened, and keeps on happening, around us?

Gradually we left you there
surrounded by the river curve
and the held-out arms,
elms under the streetlight.

These vision emergencies come
wherever we go—
blind home
coming near at unlikely places.

2

One's duty: to find a place
that grows from his part of the world—
it means leaving
certain good people.

Think: near High Trail, Colorado,
a wire follows cottonwoods
helping one to know—
like a way on trust.

That lonely strand leaves the road
depending on limbs or little poles,
and slants away,
hunting a ranch in the hills.

There, for the rest of the years,
by not going there, a person could believe
some porch looking south,
and steady in the shade—maybe you,

Rescued by how the hills
happened to arrive where they are,
depending on that wire
going to an imagined place

Where finally the way the world feels
really means how things are,
in dear detail,
by ideal light all around us.

The Wanderer Awaiting Preferment

In a world where no one knows for sure
I hold the blanket for the snow to find:
come winter, then the blizzard, then demand—
the final strategy of right, the snow
like justice over stones like bread.

"Tell us what you deserve," the whole world said.
My hands belong to cold; my voice to dust,
nobody's brother; and with a gray-eyed stare
the towns I pass return me what I give, or claim:
"Wanderer, swerve: but this is a faint command."

Only what winter gives, I claim. As trees
drink dark through roots for their peculiar grain
while meager justice applauds up through the grass,
I calm the private storm within myself.
Men should not claim, nor should they have to ask.

Vocation

This dream the world is having about itself
includes a trace on the plains of the Oregon trail,
a groove in the grass my father showed us all
one day while meadowlarks were trying to tell
something better about to happen.

I dreamed the trace to the mountains, over the hills,
and there a girl who belonged wherever she was.
But then my mother called us back to the car:
she was afraid; she always blamed the place,
the time, anything my father planned.

Now both of my parents, the long line through the plain,
the meadowlarks, the sky, the world's whole dream
remain, and I hear him say while I stand between the two,
helpless, both of them part of me:
"Your job is to find what the world is trying to be."

The Rescued
Year
1966

I

The Tulip Tree

Many a winter night
the green of the tulip tree
lives again among other trees,
returns through miles of rain
to that level of color
all day pattered, wind-wearied,
calmly asserted in our yard.

Only pale by the evergreen,
hardly distinguished by leaf or color,
it used to slide a little pale from other trees
and—no great effect at our house—
it sustained what really belonged
but would, if severely doubted,
disappear.

Many a winter night
It arrives and says for a moment.
"I am still here."

Some Shadows

You would not want too reserved a speaker—
that is a cold way to live.
But where I come from withdrawal
is easy to forgive.

When Mother was a girl Indians
shadowed that country, the barren lands.
Mother ran to school winter mornings
with hot potatoes in her hands.

She was like this—foreign, a stranger.
She could not hear very well;
the world was all far. (Were the others laughing?
She never could tell.)

Later, though she was frightened,
she loved, like everyone.
A lean man, a cruel, took her.
I am his son.

He was called Hawk by the town people,
but was an ordinary man.
He lived by trapping and hunting
wherever the old slough ran.

Our house was always quiet.
Summers the windmill creaked, or a board.
I carried wood, never touching anyone.
Winters the black stove roared.

Forgive me these shadows I cling to, good people,
trying to hold quiet in my prologue.
Hawks cling the barrens wherever I live.
The world says, "Dog eat dog."

My Father: October 1942

He picks up what he thinks is
a road map, and it is
his death: he holds it easily, and
nothing can take it from his firm hand.
The pulse in his thumb on the map
says, "1:19 P.M. next Tuesday, at
this intersection." And an ambulance
begins to throb while his face looks tired.

Any time anyone may pick up something
so right that he can't put it down:
that is the problem for all who travel—they
fatally own whatever is really theirs,
and that is the inner thread, the lock,
what can hold. If it is to be, nothing breaks
it. Millions of observers guess all the
time, but each person, once, can say, "Sure."

Then he's no longer an observer. He isn't right,
or wrong. He just wins or loses.

Back Home

The girl who used to sing in the choir
would have a slow shadow on dependable walls,
I saw. We walked summer nights.
Persons came near in those days,
both afraid but not able to know
anything but a kind of Now.

In the maples an insect sang
insane for hours about how deep the dark was.
Over the river, past the light on the bridge,
and then where the light quelled at limits
in the park, we left the town,
the church lagging pretty far behind.

When I went back I saw many sharp things:
the wild hills coming to drink at the river,
the church pondering its old meanings.
I believe the hills won; I am afraid
the girl who used to sing in the choir
broke into jagged purple glass.

Across Kansas

My family slept those level miles
but like a bell rung deep till dawn
I drove down an aisle of sound,
nothing real but in the bell,
past the town where I was born.

Once you cross a land like that
you own your face more: what the light
struck told a self; every rock
denied all the rest of the world.
We stopped at Sharon Springs and ate—

My state still dark, my dream too long to tell.

A Family Turn

All her Kamikaze friends admired my aunt,
their leader, charmed in vinegar,
a woman who could blaze with such white blasts
as Lawrence's that lit Arabia.
Her mean opinions bent her hatpins.

We'd take a ride in her old car
that ripped like Sherman through society:
Main Street's oases sheltered no one
when she pulled up at Thirty-first
and whirled that Ford for another charge.

We swept headlines from under rugs, names
all over town, which I learned her way, by heart,
and blazed with love that burns because it's real.
With a turn that's our family's own,
she'd say, "Our town is not the same"—

Pause—"And it's never been."

114

Fifteen

South of the bridge on Seventeenth
I found back of the willows one summer
day a motorcycle with engine running
as it lay on its side, ticking over
slowly in the high grass. I was fifteen.

I admired all that pulsing gleam, the
shiny flanks, the demure headlights
fringed where it lay; I led it gently
to the road and stood with that
companion, ready and friendly. I was fifteen.

We could find the end of a road, meet
the sky on out Seventeenth. I thought about
hills, and patting the handle got back a
confident opinion. On the bridge we indulged
a forward feeling, a tremble. I was fifteen.

Thinking, back farther in the grass I found
the owner, just coming to, where he had flipped
over the rail. He had blood on his hand, was pale—
I helped him walk to his machine. He ran his hand
over it, called me good man, roared away.

I stood there, fifteen.

Homecoming

Under my hat I custom you intricate, Ella;
at homecoming I glance and remember your street.
"What happened to Ella?" they ask, asking too fast;
so I fold them off, thousands of answers deep.

"Nobody saw her after the war." We are driving;
in front of the Union Building we stop and get out.
You balanced one night on that step, then leaned.
"There's Potter's Lake." And there goes our path down straight.

"Hello, Paul." "Howdy, Tom." "Glad to see you again."
They shake. "It's been a long time," they bellow, "by God!"
I shake. They sing an old song. I hunt a face.
Every voice yells in my ear, "She's married or dead."

Oh all you revelers, back of the songs you're singing
they have torn down Ella's house—you've forgotten it;
and Ella is lost, who brightened all our class,
and I stand here, home-come, to celebrate.

Under my hat I custom you intricate, Ella,
passing the places, betraying them all with a wave,
adding past dates and jobs that led us apart
flickering into revolving doors, till I've

Lost you. What happened to Ella? Where does she live?
Remember, Tom? She's that girl we once spoke of.

The Rescued Year

Take a model of the world so big
it is the world again, pass your hand,
press back that area in the west where no one lived,
the place only your mind explores. On your thumb
that smudge becomes my ignorance, a badge
the size of Colorado: toward that state by train
we crossed our state like birds and lodged—
the year my sister gracefully
grew up—against the western boundary
where my father had a job.

Time should go the way it went
that year: we weren't at war; we had
each day a treasured unimportance;
the sky existed, so did our town;
the library had books we hadn't read;
every day at school we learned and sang,
or at least hummed and walked in the hall.

116

In church I heard the preacher; he said
"Honor!" with a sound like empty silos
repeating the lesson. For a minute I held
Kansas Christian all along the Santa Fe.
My father's mean attention, though, was busy—this
I knew—and going home his wonderfully level gaze
would hold the state I liked, where little happened
and much was understood. I watched my father's finger
mark off huge eye-scans of what happened in the creed.

Like him, I tried. I still try,
send my sight like a million pickpockets
up rich people's drives; it is time
when I pass for every place I go to be alive.
Around any corner my sight is a river,
and I let it arrive: rich by those brooks
his thought poured for hours
into my hand. His creed: the greatest ownership
of all is to glance around and understand.

That Christmas Mother made paper
presents; we colored them with crayons
and hung up a tumbleweed for a tree.
A man from Hugoton brought my sister
a present (his farm was tilted near oil
wells; his car ignored the little
bumps along our drive: nothing
came of all this—it was just part of the year).

I walked out where a girl I knew would be;
we crossed the plank over the ditch
to her house. There was popcorn on the stove,
and her mother recalled the old days, inviting me back.
When I walked home in the cold evening,
snow that blessed the wheat had roved
along the highway seeking furrows,
and all the houses had their lights—
oh, that year did not escape me: I rubbed
the wonderful old lamp of our dull town.

That spring we crossed the state again,
my father soothing us with stories:
the river lost in Utah, underground—
"They've explored only the ones they've found!"—
and that old man who spent his life knowing,
unable to tell how he knew—
"I've been sure by smoke, persuaded
by mist, or a cloud, or a name:
once the truth was ready"—my father smiled
at this—"it didn't care how it came."

In all his ways I hold that rescued year—
comes that smoke like love into the broken
coal, that forms to chunks again and lies
in the earth again in its dim folds, and comes a sound,
then shapes to make a whistle fade,
and in the quiet I hold no need, no hurry:
any day the dust will move, maybe settle;
the train that left will roll back into our station,
the name carved on the platform unfill with rain,
and the sound that followed the couplings back
will ripple forward and hold the train.

Judgments

I accuse—
 Ellen: you have become forty years old,
 and successful, tall, well-groomed,
 gracious, thoughtful, a secretary.
 Ellen, I accuse.

George—
 You know how to help others;
 you manage a school. You never
 let fear or pride or faltering plans
 break your control.
 George, I accuse.

118

I accuse—
    Tom: you have found a role;
    now you meet all kinds of people
    and let them find the truth of your
    eminence; you need not push.
    Oh, Tom, I do accuse.

Remember—
    The gawky, hardly to survive students
    we were; not one of us going to succeed,
    all of us abjectly aware of how cold,
    unmanageable the real world was?
    I remember. And that fear was true.
    And is true.

Last I accuse—
    Myself: my terrible poise, knowing
    even this, knowing that then we
    sprawled in the world
    and were ourselves part of it; now
    we hold it firmly away with gracious
    gestures (like this of mine!) we've achieved.

I see it all too well—
    And I am accused, and I accuse.

Uncle George

Some catastrophes are better than others.
Wheat under the snow lived by blizzards
that massacred stock on Uncle George's farm.
Only telephone poles remember the place, and the wire
thrills a mile at a time into that intent blast
where the wind going by fascinated whole
millions of flakes and thousands of acres of tumbleweeds.

There in the spring birds will come measuring along
their nesting stream where I like to go hunt through the snow
for furred things that wait and survive. Trapper
of warm sight, I plow and belong, send breath
to be part of the day, and where it arrives
I spend on and on, fainter and fainter
toward ultimate identification, joining the air
a few breaths at a time. I test a bough
that held, last year, but this year may come down.

The cold of Uncle George's farm I carry home in my
overcoat, where I live reluctantly one life at a time;
like one driven on, I flutter, measure my stream
by many little calls: "Oh, Uncle George—where you
poured the chicken feed!—where you broke open
the window screen for the nesting swallow!—where the barn
held summer and winter against that slow blizzard, the sky!"

Aunt Mabel

This town is haunted by some good deed
that reappears like a country cousin, or truth
when language falters these days trying to lie,
because Aunt Mabel, an old lady gone now, would
accost even strangers to give bright flowers
away, quick as a striking snake. It's deeds like this
have weakened me, shaken by intermittent trust,
stricken with friendliness.

Our Senator talked like war, and Aunt Mabel
said, "He's a brilliant man,
but we didn't elect him that much."

Everyone's resolve weakens toward evening
or in a flash when a face melds—a stranger's, even—
reminded for an instant between menace and fear:
There are Aunt Mabels all over the world,
    or their graves in the rain.

120

Strokes

The left side of her world is gone—
the rest sustained by memory
and a realization: There are still the children.

Going down our porch steps her pastor
calls back: "We are proud of her recovery,
and there is a chiropractor up in Galesburg. . . ."

The birthdays of the old require such candles.

Our City Is Guarded by Automatic Rockets

1

Breaking every law except the one
for Go, rolling its porpoise way, the rocket
staggers on its course; its feelers lock
a stranglehold ahead; and—locking —finders
whispering "Target, Target," back and forth,
relocating all its meaning in the dark,
it freezes on the final stage. I know
that lift and pour, the flick out of the sky
and then the power. Power is not enough.

2

Bough touching bough, touching . . . till the shore,
a lake, an undecided river, and a lake again
saddling the divide: a world that won't be wise
and let alone, but instead is found outside
by little channels, linked by chance, not stern;
and then when once we're sure we hear a guide
it fades away toward the opposite end of the road
from home—the world goes wrong in order to have revenge.
Our lives are an amnesty given us.

121

3

There is a place behind our hill so real
it makes me turn my head, no matter. There
in the last thicket lies the cornered cat
saved by its claws, now ready to spend
all there is left of the wilderness, embracing
its blood. And that is the way that I will spit
life, at the end of any trail where I smell any hunter,
because I think our story should not end—
or go on in the dark with nobody listening.

Believer

A horse could gallop over our bridge that minnows
used for shade, but our dog trotting would splinter
that bridge—"Look down," my father said, and there
went Buster to break that bridge, but I called him back
that day:—whatever they ask me to believe, "And
    furthermore," I say.

At Niagara one night in a motel I woke, and this is what I saw—
on their little pallets all our kids lay scattered over
the floor, their dreams overcome by the story we live,
and I awake in that spell. Since then, every night
I leap through doubt, eager to find
    many more truths to tell.

And scared as I am with my blood full of sharks, I lie
in the dark and believe that whistle our dog's ears could hear
but no one else heard—it skewers my dream; and in crystals
finer than frost I trace and accept all of the ways
to know:—they tell me a lie; I don't say "But"—
    there are ways for a lie to be so.

You don't hear me yell to test the quiet or try to shake
the wall, for I understand that the wrong sound weakens
what no sound could ever save, and I am the one
to live by the hum that shivers till the world can sing:—
May my voice hover and wait for fate,
    when the right note shakes everything.

Letter from Oregon

Mother, here there are shadowy salmon;
ever their sides argue up the falls.
Watching them plunge with fluttering gills,
I thought back through Wyoming where I came from.

The gleaming sides of my train glimmered
up over passes and arrowed through shoals
of aspen fluttering in a wind of yellow.
Only the sky stayed true; I turned,

Justifying space through those miles of Wyoming
till the wave of the land was quelled by the stars;
then tunnels of shadow led me far
through doubt, and I was home.

Mother, even home was doubtful;
many slip into the sea and are gone for years,
just as I boarded the six-fifteen there.
Over the bar I have leaped outward.

Somewhere in the ocean beyond Laramie
when that grass folded low in the dark
a lost fin waved, and I felt the beat
of the old neighborhood stop, on our street.

A *Farewell* in *Tumbleweed Time*

One after another, fish fast over the fence
and quick roll to rebound, lost summer
marshaled her ragged bushy-haired children;
and pell-mell for winter, into our starved light
the west blizzard harried bigger Attila tumbleweeds
driven down what became a canyon
wherever you looked and what stood silvery
gray leaning upward—the part of the storm
you could see, your movable cell, a wild prison.

Our house then, disguised to be any house, outwaited
the storm; our mailbox in sunlight held
level; our gate steadied by shadow performed
a scenario. But into it years came, and then all that
bravery everyone praised good people for
was the wrong thing: nothing changed fast, but moss
muted every brick with its message, while
vines tried to find our grandparents' weaknesses
all up the tall chimney.

I was going to come back some day
after the fragments and I found a new home
and offer to the indifferent air a secret
no one there could use at the time:
about four some winter's day, somewhere
roads don't go, where hills come down,
I'd hold out the unfinished years of our life
and call for the steadfast rewards we were promised.
I'd speak for all the converging days of our town.

Then it would be like the flood of Christmas that
preserved every stone and set all the stars on the hill
where the farm leaned when we came out Main Street
with so much richness we couldn't ever give it away.
But all the rest of this time, after Father died, I
haven't been able to tell anyone half of the things
we carried around in that old car and couldn't say;
and there are people now I couldn't confront, even this far,
without dislodging everything in the West.

A new time is here now; I have come back,
and though I speak with less noise
all the little clods lie stunned with effort to remember,
for again it is tumbleweed time; they come to
judge us again. I know that the weakness we blame in ourselves
is in the judgment we use: I know what I remember wheels
endlessly here to say the same thing. And I know it is time
to cut loose off downwind free
like the eagles that keep the mountains clean.

II

At the Chairman's Housewarming

Talk like a jellyfish can ruin a party.
It did: I smiled whatever they said,
all the time wanting to assert myself
by announcing to all, "I eat whole wheat bread."

The jelly talk stole out on the cloth
and coated the silver tine by tine,
folding meek spoons and the true knifeblades
and rolling a tentacle into the wine.

And my talk too—it poured on the table
and coiled and died in the sugar bowl,
twitching a last thin participle
to flutter the candle over its soul.

Nothing escaped the jellyfish,
that terror from seas where whales can't live
(he could kill sharks by grabbing their tails
and neither refusing nor consenting to give).

Oh go home, you terrible fish;
let sea be sea and rock be rock.
Go back wishy-washy to your sheltered bay,
but let me live definite, shock by shock.

When I Was Young

That good river that flowed backward
when it felt the danger of Babylon
taught the rest of us in the story how to be good,
but my mother said, "God, I used to love that town."

Animals that knew the way to Heaven
wagged at the back doors of every house
when I was young, and horses told fences
the story of Black Beauty, and smelled of the good manger.

Those times tested the pre-war clocks, and
cold mornings they rang and rang. I haven't recently
seen rivers flow backward or animals that remember.
The clocks, though, still pursue what they endlessly loved.

Doubt on the Great Divide

One of the lies the world is compelled to tell
is that God grips boards by thought into Plato's table.
Better to stand in the dark of things and crash,
hark yourself, blink in the day, eat bitter bush
and look out over the world. A steadfast wire
shaking off birds into the paralyzed air
crosses the country; in the sound of noon you stand
while tethers whisper out and come to their end.

Mountains that thundered promises now say something small—
wire in the wind, and snow beginning to fall.

126

Winterward

Early in March we pitched our scar,
this fact of a life, in dust;
in summer there was a green alarm,
a foxfire of fear, the distrust
of sighting under a willow tree
a little eggshell, burst.

It was mostly quiet, but threatenings
flared wherever we looked;
in autumn the birds fell to the ground
and crawled away to the rocks;
no sleep at night for anyone,
we stared at a moon like chalk.

Now we hear the stars torn upward
out of the sky; the alarm
shadows us as we run away
from this fact of a life, our home.
Oh winter, oh snowy interior,
rocks and hurt birds, we come.

The Epitaph Ending in And

In the last storm, when hawks
blast upward and a dove is
driven into the grass, its broken wings
a delicate design, the air between
wracked thin where it stretched before,
a clear spring bent close too often
(that Earth should ever have such wings
burnt on in blind color!), this will be
good as an epitaph:

Doves did not know where to fly, and

Keepsakes

Star Guides:
> Any star is enough
> if you know what star it is.

Kids:
> They dance before they learn
> there is anything that isn't music.

The Limbs of the Pin Oak Tree:
> "Gravity—what's that?"

An Argument Against the Empirical Method:
> Some haystacks don't even have any needle.

Comfort:
> We think it is calm here,
> or that our storm is the right size.

A Documentary from America

When the Presidential candidate came to our town
he had used up his voice, but he delivered a speech
written by a committee, through a friend of his
running on the same ticket. The candidate smiled.
We cheered his courage, and a cynic hissed:
"Fools, you are on TV and have just helped elect that man!"

Later at a motel in Nanton, Alberta
(a town on the plains with a special surprise—
a pipe that gushes a drink like a flash by the road),
we tuned in a show with a variety of plots
to stalk viewers with (whereas Westerns had only
to open up with one, say a .44) there in the twilight.

In the midst of a commercial we had democratically
elected and now found delivered forever on the screen,
we were interrupted to learn we had just won a war,
certified by experts to be correct. We felt at ease,
conscience a subliminal bonus, delivered
by flags and that eerie music when the enemy appeared.

Then there was our candidate smiling at our crowd,
just as an interviewer invaded our motel to ask what program
we were watching. "Oh God," we said, "we were watching
us, watching us." And in a terrible voice he roared,
"Quick, be smiling; you are on the air again!" and—
a terrible thing—we said just as he said, "How do you do."

Out West

This air the mountains watch, in Oregon, holds
every flower or tree embraced. You meet
the air at the door and stop; it has brought
waterfalls in its breath. Kids call, dogs bark,
a chain saw climbs the latticework behind the trees.

We know each day by the space it has
and then what fills it. There is a reward
here—maybe the mountains, maybe only the sense
that after what is must come something else, always.
It's a light thing, a bounce, to live here.

At Salem we saw Governor Hatfield
wave his hand: his arm was
the taffy Oregon pulled, and his voice
was drawn by invisible birds as far
as geese bob in the reeds near Klamath Falls.

The Oregon day crowds in at the door,
its cool air and the smell of rain brought
all over as we tremble to smell
the fog in its paw, our breath moving to get
loose in the woods or over the restless water.

And in the mountains that water is clear,
only a reminder of the air it looks at;
the trout hang there on their little
fin wings, hearing the Governor speak into the
microphone spots on their applauding gills.

At This Point on the Page

Frightened at the slant of the writing, I looked up
at the student who shared it with me—
such pain was in the crossing of each t,
and a heart that skipped—lurched—in the loop of the y.
Sorrowing for the huddled lines my eyes had seen—
the terror of the o's and a's, and those draggled g's,
I looked up at her face,
not wanting to read farther, at least by prose:
the hand shook that wrote that far on the page,
and what weight formed each word, God knows.

At the Fair

Even the flaws were good—

The fat lady defining the thin man
and both bracketing the bareback princess;

Ranging through the crowd the clown
taking us all in, being extreme;

And the swain with the hangdog air
putting his trust in popcorn and cotton candy.

What more could anyone ask?
We had our money's worth.

And then besides, outside the gate,
for nothing, we met one of those lithe women—

The whirling girl, laughing with a crooked old man.

Passing Remark

In scenery I like flat country.
In life I don't like much to happen.

In personalities I like mild colorless people.
And in colors I prefer gray and brown.

My wife, a vivid girl from the mountains,
says, "Then why did you choose me?"

Mildly I lower my brown eyes—
there are so many things admirable people do not understand.

At the Klamath Berry Festival

The war chief danced the old way—
the eagle wing he held before his mouth—
and when he turned the boom-boom
stopped. He took two steps. A sociologist
was there; the Scout troop danced.
I envied him the places where he had not been.

The boom began again. Outside he heard
the stick game, and the Blackfoot gamblers
arguing at poker under lanterns.
Still-moccasined and bashful, holding
the eagle wing before his mouth,
listening and listening, he danced after others stopped.

He took two steps, the boom caught up,
the mountains rose, the still deep river
slid but never broke its quiet.
I looked back when I left:
he took two steps, he took two steps,
past the sociologist.

Near Edinburgh Castle

Wind riffles a telephone book;
rain falls on a name, maybe some president
who believes in himself and his cabinet
    —now elected by the mist.

Later, the book falls apart;
names mumble "Here," then fade.
What rain, mist, or snow elect
    they then contest into the ground.

Arrived at the castle, at the top,
in the chapel, white stone inside,
we tourists and the guard read a list
    —those dead in the war, the drowned.

My hearing catches at the wind
where it worries the flag overhead
and wears away stone while we read,
    "Their only grave is the sea."

III

Following the Markings *of Dag Hammarskjöld:*

A GATHERING OF POEMS IN THE SPIRIT
OF HIS LIFE AND WRITINGS

Prologue

You have to take the road seriously
even if it promises only perspective,
and listen to how songs learn any country,
how they arch over the snow, round out from windows,
and oh, take back the less than song, the willows
that say please, the plow lines overworked
horses leave on the field and on your mind.

These are reminders I do not care to live by,
the apparent rain, the days that forgot all
but their being, the way we leaned in the swing,
our soft arrival in the dusk when the lights
met our distance, and the lights were farms,
or stars, or trains; the lines of street lights
that came on saying "Zing."

What we bring back is what we derive from
our errors: we sweep over the ground
our detectors that show where there aren't
any mines; we stamp the earth and cry
"Betrayed—not exploded, but welcomed—a trick!"
Something has folded into this weather, the gush
a mushroom caused, and all damp land becomes
clung everywhere as the hand tries to let go.
So I try not to learn, disengage because reasons
block the next needed feeling. While others
talk, all of my tentative poems begin
to open their eyes, wistful: they could
grow better! And none carry enough
the burden you lifted, to know for us,
to fear, to act, and just to be.

A Song Demonstrators in Mexico Sing in Troubled Parts of a City

Dear ones, watching us on any street,
we come in from the country where we were alone,
and all your faces charm us, make us weep,
for the little world we share, our various home.

Think of us in Aguascalientes
listening to sad music while the rain
finds every mistake in the masonry
and caverns under the city echo ancient wrong.

We have walked those miles that make a nation,
all its hills the color of the wind,
and what we passed solicits us for kindness:
we bring you greeting from that land.

Mockingbirds can't imitate baby quail
silent in fear, quiet as a leaf,
but have to match their shadows on a stone;
and we, the poor from the country, who will soon be gone,

Bring into your whirlwind a memory of stillness,
lifted a moment and carried through the town
to honor that cavern joining all of us,
the common humanity country and city own.

A Thanksgiving for My Father

"The freezing convict wanted
back in the prison. The warden
laughed and let the storm execute
him. The wind mourned."

How often such abrupt
flakes formed around us!—
jabs of ice into lace,
daggers that appeared out of nothing,

134

So graceful the heart beat
late, could never catch up
again. You imagined a face in the
snow to burn the furnace down, and

"Once a wolf brought sticks
to a beaver—the mountains are
surely that big." Oh father, why
did you ever set your son such being!

Your life was a miracle
and could build out of shadows
anything: your restless thought
has made the world haunted;

Your memory like a snowflake forms
out of the night and comes down like
a new star all the time over wolf, storm,
woods, and millions of laces. . . .

"Once a child named 'Remember'
found a forest that wasn't trees, except
for one—named 'Doris Pine.' . . ."
Oh father, you always found the way,

But even Doris—I've never found her.

Jack London

Teeth meet on a jugular, pause, and bite:
all the world turns red but the falling snow,
and oh how quiet the river holds its flow
by one bank, then another—the vise of rock
and the force of summer fighting far below.

Another time, on an island, wedge birds
come, welcome to fly and exercise their song
on what divides all hope from land;
the sky holds where it is, but ready to move
when the forest answers softly after a storm:

He found such furs for the cold, called "Beauty,"
and "Courage" that fell through the ice, and a dog so wild
it howls the mountains higher, that howled
ages ago for us to come to the North
and exercise our song, from the island world.

The Concealment: Ishi, the Last Wild Indian

A rock, a leaf, mud, even the grass
Ishi the shadow man had to put back where it was.
In order to live he had to hide that he did.
His deep canyon he kept unmarked for the world,
and only his face became lined, because no one saw it
and it therefore didn't make any difference.

If he appeared, he died; and he was the last. Erased
footprints, berries that purify the breath, rituals
before dawn with water—even the dogs roamed a land
unspoiled by Ishi, who used to own it, with his aunt
and uncle, whose old limbs bound in willow bark finally
stopped and were hidden under the rocks, in sweet leaves.

We ought to help change that kind of premature suicide,
the existence gradually mottled away till the heartbeat
blends and the messages all go one way from the world
and disappear inward: Ishi lived. It was all right
for him to make a track. In California now where his opposites
unmistakably dwell we wander their streets

And sometimes whisper his name—
"Ishi."

Glimpses in the Woods

"Don't you want people to think well of you?"
"No—give them things, and then disappear."

That yew tree in the woods, that hermit,
that giver of bows, drinker of shade
with limbs far stronger than any need
being light, airy, and conservative,
offers a sudden glimpse out far—

That yew tree down a corridor
no one plans—useless for lumber, not even a weed,
a millionaire of disregard. Miles deep,
this earth will be rich after our time,
and yew trees quietly link through the woods. . . .

In the cold woods, I looked for this place—
beside the road and far up in the cold woods:
listeners, you have met sincere men and pretenders—
all I say is I was there and am here. Let me be
remembered only for the mud on my hands.

Listeners, I have come far to keep it from
making a difference whether I lie or
tell the truth: if incidents of my journey
sing right for you, then my mouth can abide
this communion, or I can gnaw other bones.

What ponds realize in the rain, or all of
that neglect the wilderness pours into the sky
lacking any viewer after Labor Day,
I think that, and can save it—from one glance
deep through fir woods at one dark tree;

And now into its corridor like a question,
a tunnel with one end, a mine meant
to escape from the dark, the tall days go on,
go down, and there I fall, freed on a new
level—beginning to learn for my life!

Let any feather or branch on the wind occur,
and a wind that polished the stars teach me
indifference. I have known with an edge too
clear. Yew tree, make me steadfast in my
weakness: teach me the sacred blur.

Walking the Wilderness

God is never sure He has found
the right grass. It never forgets Him.
My mother in a dream dreamed
this place, where storms drown
down or where God makes it arch to mountains,
flood with winter, stare upward at His
eye that freezes people, His zero breath
their death. In the night they lie, she
dreamed, sealed with lips to earth, who wait
at last with confidence for justice
or such firm coming as the wolverine's.

All the way into her dream and back
I walk and guard the day, since daylight broke
past guards of trees and streamed away.
Hear me, full sky, all your
lines I do not know, the roads
birds fly, the channels their lives make—
my mother in the dream dreamed
even deeper: people drowned awake,
each one staring, alone, pitiable,
come to all at once in that
dream, welcomed the more, the more
they trembled. God never notices opposition;
the deep of that dream always waits.

Snowflake designs lock; they clasp in the sky,
hold their patterns one by one, down,
spasms of loneliness, each one God's answer.
Warm human representatives may vote and
manage man; but last the blizzard will dignify
the walker, the storm hack trees to cyclone
groves, he catch the snow, his brave eye
become command, the whole night howl against
his ear, till found by dawn he
reach out to God no trembling hand.

IV

Right Now

Tonight in our secret town
wires are down. Black
lights along the street blow
steady in a wind held still.
A deaf dog listens. A girl
retreats from her gaze: her eyes
go endlessly back, a spool of shadow.

Led by my own dark I go
my unmarked everlasting round
frozen in this moment: Now
smooths all the smother, held,
wild but still. I know
so well nothing moves, arrived:
my glimpse, this town, our time.

From Eastern Oregon

Your day self shimmers at the mouth of a desert cave;
then you leave the world's problem and find
your own kind of light at the pool that glows far back
where the eye says it is dark. On the cave wall
you make not a shadow but a brightness; and you can feel
with your hands the carved story now forgotten or ignored
    by the outside, obvious mountains.

Your eyes an owl, your skin a new part of the earth,
you let obsidian flakes in the dust discover your feet
while somewhere drops of water tell a rock.
You climb out again and, consumed by light, shimmer
full contemporary being, but so thin your bones
register a skeleton along the rocks like
    an intense, interior diamond.

You carry the cave home, past Black Butte,
along the Santiam. The whole state
rides deep, and the swell of knowing it makes
yearning kelp of all you can't see.
For days your friends will be juniper, but
never again will material exist enough, clear—
    not any day, not here.

Once Men Were Created

A whistle had already loomed, outside
all encompassed ways, and its blade
hurt the ears of the dogs, then a slide
past the ears of even the sleeping men
and they were awake drowning in something
only the deaf could swim.

Some thought it was only morning, or water;
a few held their ears and ran, but it just got louder.
One hoped and flooded his head and welcomed
every leaf and tap and the whole siren of the world.
But they all crazed fell,
checked and crystallized and cold.

At the time of that cruelest music now, at age fifteen,
my schoolroom sang and almost overtopped the sound,
but our Principal came. The girl beside me
bit her fingernails, and well she might, caught helpless
that year in a room in a song in a jangle
that buffeted her dress.

Oh smooth animals that swim your easy
sound, nervous only to catch a meal or a mate—
there is another level of your mild sound, and it
scrapes with a fingernail; it has its whelps in a cave;
deeper than anyone knows it arches cathedrals,
and sends anthems like this over the grave.

Across the Lake's Eye

Walking ice across the lake's eye
to the deep and looking along the sight
at other worlds asleep for space
but not for light—
we came wide awake.
"Why close what eyes we have?" you said,

And "There's a left-hand world that other people see
that slinks aside from me,
that my dog hears;
the negative of the world, that suicides love;
that comes along the track from its pinpoint place;
that barely swerves beside our face
escaping either way outside our own,
beyond where night surprises the snow."

You made me look around that night.
And coming back you spun this left-hand story:
An island burrowed under the water
and rose pretending to be a different island
but a fish had followed it, making bubbles
wherever the island went. "Echoes,"
you said, "avoid that island now:
sound is dead there, but haunts the concave water
where the island used to be."

The world has character, you contended,
as we stamped home across the land,
making a record of that night,
marking the progress of an island.

A Human Condition

If there is a forest anywhere
the one you live with whimpers in her
sleep or construes a glance wrong, awake:
without intent she falls toward zero
impact; like an indicator on a chart
she rounds into terror, and the wild trees
try for her throat,
   if there is a forest anywhere.

If you concur with a world that has forests
in it, the one you live with will indict
you. If you like a farm, it will threaten.
Some people casually help each other:
if one likes a place the other finds
a kind going out of the breath at evening there.
   At your house any forest is everywhere.

But there are farms—to see them in the evening
extends your breath; you hover their hills
with regard for a world that offers human beings
a lavish, a deepening abode, in the evening,
like them. These places could have been home,
are lost to you now. They are foreign but good.
   There are these farms.

For the Grave of Daniel Boone

The farther he went the farther home grew.
Kentucky became another room;
the mansion arched over the Mississippi;
flowers were spread all over the floor.
He traced ahead a deepening home,
and better, with goldenrod:

Leaving the snakeskin of place after place,
going on—after the trees

the grass, a bird flying after a song.
Rifle so level, sighting so well
his picture freezes down to now,
a story-picture for children.

They go over the velvet falls
into the tapestry of his time,
heirs to the landscape, feeling no jar:
it is like evening; they are the quail
surrounding his fire, coming in for the kill;
their little feet move sacred sand.

Children, we live in a barbwire time
but like to follow the old hands back—
the ring in the light, the knuckle, the palm,
all the way to Daniel Boone,
hunting our own kind of deepening home.
From the land that was his I heft this rock.

Here on his grave I put it down.

Hunting

What the keen hound followed
rose in the mind for me
taller for being faint, brought
near by what might be,
till—reversal—through the world
I found so misty a trail
that all not you cried, "You!"
like a wedding bell.

Bugles that fade are still bugles;
birds that sang wait still:
deep in the woods is that far place
once near, and our own, and real.

Sophocles Says

History is a story God is telling,
by means of hidden meanings written closely
inside the skins of things. Far over the sun
lonesome curves are meeting, and in the clouds
birds bend the wind. Hunting a rendezvous,
soft as snowflakes ride through a storm their pattern down,
men hesitate a step, touched by home.

A man passes among strangers; he never smiles;
the way a flame goes begging among the trees
he goes, and he suffers, himself, the kind of dark
that anything sent from God experiences,
until he finds through trees the lights of a town—
a street, the houses blinded in the rain—
and he hesitates a step, shocked—at home.

For God will take a man, no matter where,
and make some scene a part of what goes on:
there will be a flame; there will be a snowflake form;
and riding with the birds, wherever they are,
bending the wind, finding a rendezvous
beyond the sun or under the earth—that man
will hesitate a step—and meet his home.

Near

Walking along in this not quite prose way
we both know it is not quite prose we speak,
and it is time to notice this intolerable snow
innumerably touching, before we sink.

It is time to notice, I say, the freezing snow
hesitating toward us from its gray heaven;
listen—it is falling not quite silently
and under it still you and I are walking.

144

Maybe there are trumpets in the houses we pass
and a redbird watching from an evergreen—
but nothing will happen until we pause
to flame what we know, before any signal's given.

Recoil

The bow bent remembers home long,
the years of its tree, the whine
of wind all night conditioning
it, and its answer—Twang!

To the people here who would fret me down
their way and make me bend:
*By remembering hard I could startle for home
and be myself again.*

The Animal That Drank Up Sound

1

One day across the lake where echoes come now
an animal that needed sound came down. He gazed
enormously, and instead of making any, he took
away from, sound: the lake and all the land
went dumb. A fish that jumped went back like a knife,
and the water died. In all the wilderness around he
drained the rustle from the leaves into the mountainside
and folded a quilt over the rocks, getting ready
to store everything the place had known; he buried—
thousands of autumns deep—the noise that used to come there.

Then that animal wandered on and began to drink
the sound out of all the valleys—the croak of toads,
and all the little shiny noise grass blades make.
He drank till winter, and then looked out one night
at the stilled places guaranteed around by frozen
peaks and held in the shallow pools of starlight.
It was finally tall and still, and he stopped on the highest
ridge, just where the cold sky fell away
like a perpetual curve, and from there he walked on silently,
and began to starve.

When the moon drifted over that night the whole world lay
just like the moon, shining back that still
silver, and the moon saw its own animal dead
on the snow, its dark absorbent paws and quiet
muzzle, and thick, velvet, deep fur.

2

After the animal that drank sound died, the world
lay still and cold for months, and the moon yearned
and explored, letting its dead light float down
the west walls of canyons and then climb its delighted
soundless way up the east side. The moon
owned the earth its animal had faithfully explored.
The sun disregarded the life it used to warm.

But on the north side of a mountain, deep in some rocks,
a cricket slept. It had been hiding when that animal
passed, and as spring came again this cricket waited,
afraid to crawl out into the heavy stillness.
Think how deep the cricket felt, lost there
in such a silence—the grass, the leaves, the water,
the stilled animals all depending on such a little
thing. But softly it tried—"Cricket!"—and back like a river
from that one act flowed the kind of world we know,
first whisperings, then moves in the grass and leaves;
the water splashed, and a big night bird screamed.

It all returned, our precious world with its life and sound,
where sometimes loud over the hill the moon,
wild again, looks for its animal to roam, still,
down out of the hills, any time.
But somewhere a cricket waits.

It listens now, and practices at night.

Read to the Last Line

Suppose a heroic deed—
at a big picnic, say, you save a child;
later the child is killed while being a hero;
then you meet the beautiful sister,
and all . . . ; you have a son who wakes
in the middle of the night and cries;
you hear him—strange—there in the dark, and—

Suppose all the supposes.
You find your self-story patch-quilted
all over the place; and after that
you are reading an author who tells
your whole story, around all the spirals,
till you come face to face and recognize you.

Grateful, you find yourself
identified, so clearly named that you decide
to bring other patches together by
rounding on that author, too, with some
greatest, ultimate deed: he deserves something.

So you in turn begin a story,
but then you stop—what goes on?
"I'll not tell nor be told what I think," you cry,
"None of it's true, anyway."

And all the time it's your own story,
even when you think: "It's all just made up, a trick.
What is the author trying to do?"

Reader, we are in such a story:
all of this is trying to arrange a kind of a prayer for you.

Pray for me.

Allegiances
1970

This Book

Late, at the beginning of cold,
you push your breath toward home.
Silence waits at the door.
You stamp, go in, start the fire—
from any part of the room I suddenly say,
"Hello," but do not get in your way.

Quiet as all books, I wait, and promise
we'll watch the night: you turn a page;
winter misses a stride. You see
the reason for time, for everything in the sky.
And into your eyes I climb, on the strongest
thread in the world, weaving the dark and the cold.

I

With Kit, Age 7, at the Beach

We would climb the highest dune,
from there to gaze and come down:
the ocean was performing;
we contributed our climb.

Waves leapfrogged and came
straight out of the storm.
What should our gaze mean?
Kit waited for me to decide.

Standing on such a hill,
what would you tell your child?
That was an absolute vista.
Those waves raced far, and cold.

"How far could you swim, Daddy,
in such a storm?"
"As far as was needed," I said,
and as I talked, I swam.

Bess

Ours are the streets where Bess first met her
cancer. She went to work every day past the
secure houses. At her job in the library
she arranged better and better flowers, and when
students asked for books her hand went out
to help. In the last year of her life
she had to keep her friends from knowing
how happy they were. She listened while they
complained about food or work or the weather.
And the great national events danced
their grotesque, fake importance. Always

Pain moved where she moved. She walked
ahead; it came. She hid; it found her.
No one ever served another so truly;
no enemy ever meant so strong a hate.
It was almost as if there was no room
left for her on earth. But she remembered
where joy used to live. She straightened its flowers;
she did not weep when she passed its houses;
and when finally she pulled into a tiny corner
and slipped from pain, her hand opened
again, and the streets opened, and she wished all well.

Monuments for a Friendly Girl
at a Tenth Grade Party

The only relics left are those long
spangled seconds our school clock chipped out
when you crossed the social hall
and we found each other alive,
by our glances never to accept our town's
ways, torture for advancement,
nor ever again be prisoners by choice.

Now I learn you died
serving among the natives of Garden City,
Kansas, part of a Peace Corps
before governments thought of it.

Ruth, over the horizon your friends eat
foreign chaff and have addresses like titles,
but for you the crows and hawks patrol
the old river. May they never
forsake you, nor you need monuments
other than this I make, and the one
I hear clocks chip in that world we found.

Holcomb, Kansas

The city man got dust on his shoes and carried
a box of dirt back to his apartment.
He joined the killers in jail and saw things
their way. He visited the scene of the crime
and backed people against the wall with his typewriter
and watched them squirm. He saw how it was.
And they—they saw how it was: he was
a young man who had wandered onto the farm
and begun to badger the homefolk.
So they told him stories for weeks while he
fermented the facts in his little notebook.

153

Now the wide country has gone sober again.
The river talks all through the night, proving
its gravel. The valley climbs back into its hammock
below the mountains and becomes again only what
it is: night lights on farms make little blue domes
above them, bright pools for the stars; again
people can visit each other, talk easily,
deal with real killers only when they come.

A Gesture Toward an Unfound Renaissance

There was the slow girl in art class,
less able to say where our lessons led: we
learned so fast she could not follow us.
But at the door each day I looked back
at her rich distress, knowing almost enough
to find a better art inside the lesson.

And then, late at night, when the whole town
was alone, the current below the rumbly bridge
at Main Street would go an extra swirl
and gurgle, once, by the pilings;
and at my desk at home, or when our house
opened above my bed toward the stars,
I would hear that one intended lonely sound,
the signature of the day, the ratchet of time
taking me a step toward here, now, and this
look back through the door that always closes.

Reaching out to Turn on a Light

Every lamp that approves its foot
shyly reminds of how Ellen stood.

Every bowl, every shadow that leans forth,
hunts vaguely for the pattern by her door.

154

One summer, I remember, a giant beautiful cloud
stood beyond the hill where Ellen lived.

It has been years, and we hardly looked back;
now, except for times like this, we hardly ever look.

There may be losses too great to understand
that rove after you and—faint and terrible—
    rip unknown through your hand.

Remembering Althea

When you came out of your house
and put your hand on the August day,
walls of the barn delicate in the light
began the season that would ribbon away
all that we saw and blow it past the world,

For after we contended at school, we had
our war, sought outward for enemies, awarded
each other greatness; and you were left
forgotten awhile: why touch what was
already ours, when there was more—cities, glory?

For you held no power, Althea,
according to any of us; but after the others
asserted, claimed their place, posed for
every storm, your true beam found all. That
August day is yours, and every honor

You gave away. I remember Jeff,
who always won, and Ben, and his sister,
that whole class: they are only your chorus,
because you waved and it was far and the end,
you knew, delicately, through amber, that August day.

The Last Day

To Geronimo rocks were the truth,
water less, air not at all;
but the opposite he had to learn:
his hollow hand, his nothing breath—
they filled the world when all his loss
was a place to hide. These cliffs
where he lived, those miles of stone—
relief came when they drifted across
his lightest thought; and he bought
his life in those dead hills
by the way they leaned as he touched
their sides and loved the air.

Then he could fall.

At the Grave of My Brother

The mirror cared less and less at the last, but
the tone of his voice roamed, had more to find,
back to the year he was born; and the world
that saw him awhile again went blind.

Drawn backward along the street, he disappeared
by the cedars that faded a long time ago
near the grave where Mother's hair was a screen
but she was crying. I see a sparrow

Chubby like him, full of promise, barely
holding a branch and ready to fly.
In his house today his children begin
to recede from this year and go their own way.

Brother: Good-bye.

Father's Voice

"No need to get home early;
the car can see in the dark."
        He wanted me to be rich
        the only way we could,
        easy with what we had.

And always that was his gift,
given for me ever since,
        easy gift, a wind
        that keeps on blowing for flowers
        or birds wherever I look.

World, I am your slow guest,
one of the common things
        that move in the sun and have
        close, reliable friends
        in the earth, in the air, in the rock.

Observation Car and Cigar

Tranquility as his breath, his eye a camera
that believes, he follows rails that only last
one trip, then vanish. (Suppose America
tried and then was the West once more, but this time
no one found it? He has felt that much
alone.) Remembering with smoke, he uses
the haze as authentic (the authentic loves not kept
for display fade authentically and become
priceless, never to be exchanged). A silver
evening light follows the train silently
over a great bridge. Like a camera that
believes, he follows an arch into faded
authentic scenes that bring something presented again
and yet all new: traveling, our loves are brought
before us and followed securely into a new evening.

In Sublette's Barn

I

Sublette moved up the Cimarron alert
all day for hostiles; he feared what he was finding:
no one had reported this place; once you made
camp it was time to move—it soon felt old.
He had always been the kind of man who had
the kind of horses that would turn
to look at you. In talk he listened to the current,
not the words. Now, he heard something in the country.
Maybe he had listened too long.

His friends had scattered, far valleys, not anywhere
the right place—how could it be?—or the wrong either:
Scatter. But for him the earth had lent itself, was
always his. Steady now, he still did not start any bluff moves:
what would happen was what he would intend, though the world
would swerve sometime, and his hand would miss the handle.
By his campfire, his own tea——warm or cool—was what he would
deserve. He carried an extra cup.

II

But he was lost a new way that winter, began to find
tracks he could read better and better, till all
he found went out and intensified the valley:
he came around the Cimarron breaks into a land that
began to tense itself all day for deliberate snow.
He camped there well but was afraid: once that place
was found, the West had come; no one could undiscover it.
Like a badger by that stream—so strong the trap that
grabbed his feet was bent, with his teeth grooved on everything
he bit, and miles ringed all around, so target was the place,
where—now—the sky kept saying out and out because
its color would never be at all but what it was—he took
his paw back from the steel, and watched the trap.

III

The river stopped, for him; the clouds were holding
there: Sublette's big valley crossed by trails that
surfaced under a round reminder of gold or copper sun,
shimmered toward him. He looked across a place the air
filled—saved only by his weakness, forms of monotony, meanings
that made the world regular enough to offer choices.
He had not stopped until the West climbed in at him;
but now it was the last available ranch, a place that still says:

> You never told a friend, even, a lie. You
> never tried for the good feeling you get from overvaluing
> something that's yours—indulgence that seems austere.
> It is not. You were the one who always began on the level part,
> forth on a line trued for accepted real things,
> looking across the prairies a rod of steady light.

Held where the sky touched land along the edge,
his trail encountered all his eye grooved, and went on.
Reluctant hero, he had let one deed at a time take him;
then where he was, was everywhere: the kind of trip he
took turned into carving; the knifeblade led, the hand
reluctant but so steady it was always at the place
it should be and with force as if the earth turned
for his body and the light held back until his eyes
met it, all equal, all come right at once.
His fate was righteousness.

IV

That was his land, but no one there to know. By
following him we blunder into it. Here now, fall or winter,
anytime, it's here. You move your hand across
till the fingers frame a certain line trees make by the
river always there: that's the way the man Sublette became.
Reluctantly he found and kept on finding himself the man
the land meant. It subsided and became a state.

Now snow terms are imposed for us; the wind climbs
around the barn. Eyes level—rafter, higher, window
defense above the storm—we climb, years of soft dust
molded—rafter, stanchions, haymow. No one can sound
the deep rope to those days, hold level the wide ranch
that swung in his life in his mind, Sublette's held level
way, no undeserved lunge in his kind of gaze.

What he kept may fit a box put carelessly away,
but he heard some string that sang the wilderness,
monuments that pledge the rock they come from,
statues that regret their edge—and it all goes on.
Surveillance—his assignment—brings him back to us;
our work is to forget in time what if remembered might block
that great requirement which waits on its wide wings: the
wilderness. That man—fugitive from speed, antagonist of greatness—
comes here quietly still lost, trying to tell us what he means.

Carols Back Then: 1935

Clouds on the hills. I hear a throat voice,
chiming like Ella's from that quicksand year
soon to be gone if I do not recall
the cold and the carols that rang Christmas there.

Walls are closing round that corner scene,
the street turning to iron where we sang like a bell,
and even our classmates are shrugging away.
I stand on the curb and remember it all—

That song, the star that came near and stayed,
the hulking town we walked through that night.
I can turn to it, being true to the sign,
quietly insisting with all of my life,

That life those around me now can't know.
Ella, our town is all filling with snow!

160

Some Autumn Characters

I

Rain finds lost beach toys, on
open autumn days displays them
to stare through their sky window
while uninhabited islands hear crisp Rain
come toward them, their caretaker all winter
everywhere in the woods trying
to fasten down the leaves.

II

Cold, a character I used to know
in Wyoming, raps every night
at doors of lonely farms, moans
all night around the barn, and cracks
his knuckles late, late,
at the bedroom window.

III

And One Afternoon each year
is yours. It stands again
across a certain field and is the same—
a day no year can hold, but always
warm, paused in the light, looking
back and forward, where everything counts
and every bush, tree, field, or
friend will always wave.

The Girl Engaged to the Boy Who Died

A part of the wind goes around her face,
and a part still leans where the old wind
came past the radiator cap, and held
the town gently for inspection, for
years, against the cracked windshield.

A part of the room around her chair
holds like that rock at the waterfall
where floods in the park learned
the spring rules; now the trained world,
terrifying, for years, does not
come in to disturb her hair.

A part of her eye waits for a figure
that spun close in the breath she blew
at the birthday candles, and the smoke
for years wandered into corners and waited
while packages crackled in impatient hands.

And the whole sky sprang onto her blue
umbrella she held over her head when she
ran home alone, after graduation, and saw
the yard and the dingy door of her house,
and the weeds in the drive, for years.

Strangers

Brown in the snow, a car with a heater
in it searches country roads all yesterday afternoon
for our farm. At crossroads the car stops
and over the map the two people bend.
They love how the roads go on, how the heater
hums. They are so happy they can be
lost forever that afternoon.

They will probably live.
They may die. The roads go on. On the
checkered map they find themselves, and their
car is enough audience, their eyes enough
to know. If the state breaks off they will
burrow at the edge, or fall. I thought of
them yesterday, and last night sang by the
fire, thinking of them.

They are something of us, but I think better,
lost back there in our old brown car.

The Preacher at the Corner

He talked like an old gun killing buffalo,
and in what he said a giant was trying to get out;
so I listened—breathing, harkening, hearing his foghorn,
learning; for the way I found him is the way I like:
to wander because I know the road,
and find stray things, wherever they come from.

He wasn't confident: "Many a time it's bad," he said;
"I've wanted to find a hole and pull the hole
in after me." I knew that kind of dark
a radio feels, fading, or what now and then rises
toward fear in sleep: this was a man I sought, I knew—
such a target shoots out what it is at me.

Into a pass one snowy night this man
had gone among the mountains like a mild wide sound
hunting a particular way to be lost, but he came out
on a spur and knew exactly which way north was:
"And that is exactly the trouble with you," he said.
He was looking at me: "That is exactly the trouble with you."

True, I've committed innumerable sacred crimes
and followed secret paths patrolled by ivy. Unavoidable
hills have made me stern, determined not to be wavery;
so I located this man, sure enough, considerably south.
But had he glimpsed a wonderful, possible confusion?—
a strange kind of turn in the path, a kind of ivy?

The Gift

The writer's home he salvages from little pieces
along the roads, from distinctions he remembers,
from what by chance he sees—his grabbed heritage;
and from people fading from his road, from history.
He reaches out far, being a desperate man;
he comprehends by fistfuls with both hands.
But what can bring in enough to save the tame
or be home for them who even with roofs are shelterless?

We give them scenes like this:
a tree that blooms in a gale, a stone
the gale can't move, a breath song
against the pane from outside,
breathing, "Some day, tame (therefore lost) men, the wild
will come over the highest wall, waving
its banner voice, beating its gifted fist:
Begin again, you tame ones; listen—the roads are your home again."

II

Return to Single-Shot

(The John Day Country)

People who come back refuse to touch
what has been theirs, and in their speech
they give the words a twist, a foreign sound.
Cautiously they walk, wanting all they find
this time to be something else, for someone else.
Then each comes to a stop before the house
longest his, and in his perfect speech
repeats: "This is my house, and I am
still myself." And that restarts the town.

Their fingers find again the grain of wood;
they memorize the promise of the land:
what curves reliably comes back right;
to a fence, responsibility is not obsolete.
One aims a single-shot and hears the muffled past
interject that old, flat, simple sound—
the name of Daniel Boone's psychiatrist.

Remember—

The little towns day found
flowing down streets held still,
and the quiet way we lay there then,
waking?

That sheep town, say, in Nevada
where bells woke us in the dark
and we followed the ditch to a willow—
one, green?

That was almost, through quiet, the time:
the world stilled for dawn,
that instant belonged to the world.
We were there.

Coming back was toward strong light;
the town lay. Nothing was new;
still, the horizon gained something
more than color.

Out there beyond grasp was the air,
and beyond the air was a touch
any morning could bring us—
any morning.

Behind the Falls

First the falls, then the cave:
then sheets of sound around us fell
while earth fled inward, where we went.
We traced it back, cigarette lighter high—
lost the roof, then the wall,
found abruptly in that space
only the flame and ourselves,
and heard the curtain like the earth
go down, so still it made the lighter
dim that led us on under the hill.

We stopped, afraid—lost
if ever that flame went out—
and surfaced in each other's eyes,
two real people suddenly
more immediate in the dark
than in the sun we'd ever be.
When men and women meet that way
the curtain of the earth descends, and they
find how faint the light has been, how far
mere honesty or justice is from all they need.

Montana Eclogue

I

After the fall drive, the last
horseman humps down the trail south;
High Valley turns into a remote, still cathedral.
Stone Creek in its low bank turns calmly
through the trampled meadow. The one scouting
thunderhead above Long Top hangs to watch,
ready for its reinforcement due in October.

Logue, the man who always closes down the camp,
is left all alone at Clear Lake, where
he is leisurely but busy, pausing to glance across
the water toward Winter Peak. The bunkhouse
will be boarded up, the cookshack barricaded
against bears, the corral gates lashed shut.
Whatever winter needs, it will have to find
for itself, all the slow months the wind owns.

From that shore below the mountain the water
darkens; the whole surface of the lake livens,
and, upward, high miles of pine tops bend where a storm
walks the country. Deeper and deeper, autumn
floods in. Nothing can hold against that current
the aspens feel. And Logue, by being there, suddenly
carries for us everything that we can load on him,
we who have stopped indoors and let our faces
forget how storms come: that lonely man works for us.

II

Far from where we are, air owns those ranches
our trees hardly hear of, open places
braced against cold hills. Mornings, that
news hits the leaves like rain, and we
stop everything time brings, and freeze that one,
open, great, real thing—the world's gift: day.

Up there, air like an axe chops, near timberline,
the clear-cut miles the marmots own. We
try to know, all deep, all sharp, even while
busy here, that other: gripped in a job,
aimed steady at a page, or riffled by distractions,
we break free into that world of the farthest coat—air

We glimpse that last storm when the wolves
get the mountains back, when our homes will flicker
bright, then dull, then old; and the trees
will advance, knuckling their roots or lying in
windrows to match the years. We glimpse
a crack that begins to run down the wall,
and like a blanket over the window at night
that world is with us and those wolves are here.

III

Up there, ready to be part of what comes, the high lakes
lie in their magnificent beds; but men,
great as their heroes are, live by their deeds
only as a pin of shadow in a cavern their thought
gets lost in. We pause; we stand where
we are meant to be, waver as foolish as
we are, tell our lies with all the beautiful grace
an animal has when it runs—

*Citizen, step back from the fire and let night
have your head: suddenly you more than hear
what is true so abruptly that God is cold:—
winter is here. What no one saw, has
come. Then everything the sun approved could
really fail? Shed from your back, the years
fall one by one, and nothing that comes
will be your fault. You breathe a few breaths
free at the thought: things can come so great
that your part is too small to count,
if winter can come.*

Logue brings us all that. Earth took
the old saints, who battered their hearts,
met arrows, or died by the germs God sent;
but Logue, by being alone and occurring to us,
carries us forward a little,
and on his way out for the year will
stand by the shore and see winter in,
the great, repeated lesson every year.

A storm bends by that shore and
one flake at a time teaches grace,
even to stone.

A Story

After they passed I climbed
out of my hole and sat
in the sun again. Loose rocks
all around make it safe—I can
hear anyone moving. It often
troubles me to think how others
dare live where stealth is possible,
and how they can feel safe, considering
all the narrow places,
without whiskers.

Anyway, those climbers were a puzzle—
above where I live nothing lives.
And they never came down. There is no
other way. The way it is,
they crawl far before they die.
I make my hole the deepest one
this high on the mountainside.

A Memorial Day

Said a blind fish loved that lake—
big one, doggo at the deepest place,
whiskered with scorn at any lure or bait.
Hugo said this, leading us
the road he chose years ago, to Price's Lake,
a stout authority.

He remembered this turn, that,
a rock, the way the road asked
"Where? Where?"
I watched his face swept by cat's-paws
when we found the camp tumbledown,
and back of cabins drunken Chryslers,
Hudsons even—old elephants—fallen
on alder swords through their ribs.

When winter strikes, that camp sinks
till spring, and every year
the moss gains and willows cringe
more. Coming out, our car, strong
under its hood, growled where those
old cars gasped—"Those heroes,"
Hugo said, with respect:
"I don't much go for chrome."

Quiet Town

Here in our cloud we talk
baking powder. Our yeast feet
make tracks that fill up with fog.
Tongue like a sponge, we describe
the air that we eat—how it has its own
lungs, inhales many a stranger.

Our stories have executives who flash
ornamental knives. Their children use them
afternoons to toast marshmallows.
Technicians in suicide plan courses
in high school for as long as it takes.

For our gestures, feathers are emphatic
enough; a snowflake smashes through
revealed rock. Our town balances,
and we have a railroad. Pitiful bandits
who storm the bank are led away,
their dreamy guns kicked into the gutter
by kids coming out of the movie.

No one is allowed to cross our lake at night.
Every Christmas we forget by selective remembering.
Overhead planes mutter our fear
and are dangerous, are bombs exploding
a long time, carrying bombs elsewhere to explode.

170

A Letter

DEAR GOVERNOR:
     Rather than advise you this time or complain
I will report on one of our little towns
where I stopped last week at evening.
This town has no needs. Not one person stirred
by the three lights on Main Street. It lay
so mild and lost that I wanted you to know
how some part of your trust appears, too far
or too dim to demand or be afraid.
Now I let it all go back into its mist from
the silent river. Maybe no one will
report it to you any more.

     You could think of that place annually
on this date, for reassurance—a place where we
have done no wrong. For these days to find out
what to forgive one must listen and watch:
even our friends draft us like vampires, and it is
the non-localized hurts that do the damage.
We have to forgive carefully those demands
for little helps, those unhappy acquaintances.
We must manage the ultimate necessary withdrawal
somehow, sometimes let the atoms swirl by.

     So, this time, please keep on being the way
you are, and think of that town. A locust tree
put its fronds, by the way, quietly into the
streetlight; repeated breaths of river wind
came up-canyon. Let that—the nothing, the no one,
the calm night——often recur to you.

Sincerely,
A Friend

A Sound from the Earth

Somewhere, I think in Dakota,
they found the leg bones—just the
big leg bones—of several hundred
buffalo, in a gravel pit.

Near there, a hole in a cliff
has been hollowed so that
the prevailing wind
thrums a note so low and persistent
that bowls of water placed in that
cave will tremble to foam.

The grandfather of Crazy Horse
lived there, they say, at the last,
and his voice like the thrum of the hills
made winter come as he sang, "Boy,
where was your buffalo medicine?
I say you were not brave enough, Boy.
I say Crazy Horse was too cautious."

Then the sound he cried out for his grandson
made that thin Agency soup that they
put before him tremble. The whole
earthen bowl churned into foam.

Flowers at an Airport

Part of the time sun, part of
the time shade, a limousine slides
the airport drive; the driver
gets out and stands by the curb: sun.
*When they look back at our day and
ask their charts, they'll say
there never was such a time.*

This is the Governor's man, to
take the Governor home. *What picks
us off is time: Martin Luther
King, soldiers on patrol, kids
protected at home, the young,
the old, Lurleen.*

It is a quiet day. The time is
anyone's clock—seconds like
pomegranate seeds. The man
looks over the day. *Outside
what anyone knows, grackles
make a sound that imitates reeds;
their wings hover this air
that spills across the field.*

This is our time. We stand
inside a curve, inside long lines
that make a more secret curve.
We hear wind through the grass.
*Shadows that live in these roses fall
through thorns and become
shares in what lasts and lasts.*

Texas—

Wide, no limit, the whole
state an airport, a continent
marbles could roll across; and
they say when the fist of the sun
hammers it, the natives love it,
feel they would die if moved. They
have struggled to stay, and have
won, a catastrophe. Now they deserve it–
a cruel thing to say. But true.

But wide. I came on the Sweetwater
once. It was evening, and the doves
insisted they could redeem all the
universe. Never after that could I
deny a link with Texas. A farmer
strikes oil, and stuffs his mattress
with money, like excelsior. At a
space lab they look around and think,
"Might as well try for the moon."

And they get there. Long ago
the rest of the country joined their state
and thus became, really, a part of Mexico—
why contend? Joining is better, and is done
many ways, even if politicians have limits.
I say join the state, and Mexico, and the
politicians. Beyond irony is the hard country
no one can misjudge, where we survive
our indulgences and mean just the earth again—

Texas

Garden City

That town, those days, composed grand
arching pictures down by the river.
A cloud or a girl strayed by. Any storm
was temporary. Those hills to the south
rush into the lens, emboss the world;
and I can see so well that the hawks grow
pin feathers. Our class picnic
blossoms in ribbons and watermelon.

Sophomores of that year, you innocent swimmers
dissolved hundreds of times in my prayers:
the world we studied has taken us; it
opened its afternoons deep as a pond. But sometimes

174

Main Street at midnight flashes its fin,
or for a moment, over our days, over such
indignities as time gave us all for our share,
the monstrous blue fender of Stocky's old Hudson
reels down the white line toward home.

Memorials of a Tour Around Mt. Hood

I

At a Pioneer Cemetery

Both sides fought stillness
but stillness came:
flintlock, war cry—
now no name.

Dust holds them; restful
grass grows high:
together they grapple
the real enemy.

Overhead, fighting to break the sky,
planes trace our permanence today:
they can't go fast enough
not to go away.

II

The Cage at the Filling Station

In the turn of neck a wolverine offered
over one shoulder for his lost freedom, the world said,
Smoke ought to have a home.

175

People were talking; the wolverine
listened clear back to his tail. His body said,
Remember homeless ones.

These discontinuous gestures resting
their paws on a wall follow the thoughtful
who turn, alerted for an instant:

Smoke really ought to have a home.

III

Camping at Lost Lake

Earth at large in constellations
wafts all night our fire; and we
through the still hours feel morning
coming nearer stealthily.

Night birds flit. Darkness
takes them. Forest gulfs them all.
Our stranger eyes look for those birds
but lose them where the trees go tall.

Of course our call can't stop a bird
among those tree trunks fern has found:
our hands go out to say good-bye
as unassertive as a frond.

Among these trees till morning comes
we sleep, and dream thunders of fern
alerting space by the way they wait,
eloquent of light's return.

IV

And That Picnic at Zigzag

Tea at a campfire,
talk under the wind—
that was minimum living, Friend.

176

"Woe!" the wind cried;
"Hey!"—the light spied
what in the underbrush the chickadees did.

Well, we're older.
And the woods are colder.
But that was good tea, Friend.

Stories from Kansas

Little bunches of
grass pretend they are bushes
that never will bow.
    They bow.

Carelessly the earth
escapes, loping out from the
timid little towns
    toward Colorado.

Which of the horses
we passed yesterday whinnied
all night in my dreams?
    I want that one.

III

Things That Happen

Sometimes before great events a person will try,
disguised, at his best, not to be a clown:
he feels, "A great event is coming, bow down."
And I, always looking for something anyway,
always bow down.

Once, later than dawn but early,
before the lines of the calendar fell,
one of those events turned an unseen corner
and came near, near, sounding before it
something the opposite from a leper's bell.

We were back of three mountains called
"Sisters" along the Green Lakes trail
and had crossed a ridge when that
one little puff of air touched us,
hardly felt at all.

That was the greatest event that day;
it righted all wrong.
I remember it, the way the dust moved there.
Something had come out of the ground
and moved calmly along.

No one was ahead of us, no one
in all that moon-like land.
Oh, I thought, how hard the world has tried
with its wind, its miles, its blundering
stumbling days, again and again, to find my hand.

Christianite

This new kind of metal will not suffer:
it either holds or bends.
Under stress it acts like a bar, or a hinge.

This metal possesses a lucky way,
always to respond by endurance, or
an eager collapse, and forget.

(The time between the loss and the end
costs all the wear: earlier,
you win; after, you start again.)

The new metal is never in-between.
You think with it, make models,
save it for when you retire.

The impulsive cannot understand it.
Only something romantic or brittle
belongs in their hands.

What I Heard Whispered at the Edge of Liberal, Kansas

Air waits for us
after we fall. It comes
perfectly together, just as a lake
does, in its every share giving
the fish paths as long
as they last. For us,
air contains all. After
we fall it waits. At the last
it is frantic with its hands
but cannot find us.
Was it a friend? Now,
too late, we think it was.

That's why we became grass.

On Don Quixote's Horse

Loose reins, the pony finds
easy trails, obvious valleys
that the grass found like birdseed,

Where thinking high we thought
hero grass around rocks
where the highest pony couldn't live.

More than valleys could be,
and air the air dreams, ponies that find other
than possible trails, thoughts like birdseed.

Walk like stilts, thought, then;
or snakelike bend, run, stand:
I call you Phantom, thought—

Trained not to be trained.

Vacation Trip

The loudest sound in our car
was Mother being glum:

> Little chiding valves
> a surge of detergent oil
> all that deep chaos
> the relentless accurate fire
> the drive shaft wild to arrive

And tugging along behind in its great big
balloon,
that looming piece of her mind:

"I wish I hadn't come."

Like a Little Stone

Like a little stone, feel the shadow of the great earth;
let distance pierce you till you cling to trees.
That the world may be all the same,
close your eyes till everything is,
    and the farthest sand can vote.

Making the world be big by hunting its opposite,
go out gleaning for lost lions
that are terrified by valleys of still lambs,
for hummingbirds that dream before each wingbeat,
    for the mole that met the sun.

If time won't let a thing happen, hurry there,
to the little end of the cone that darkness bends.
Any place where you turn but might have gone on,
all possibilities need you there.
    The centers of stones need your prayers.

Note

straw, feathers, dust—
little things

but if they all go one way,
that's the way the wind goes.

Space Country

As usual the highest birds first
caught it, a slow roll even the air
hardly felt; then the thick gold haze
that many filters of eyes found
fell deep in the desert country. Wells filled
and rocks—pooled in their own shadows—
lay at ease. People did not know
why they stood up and walked, and
waited by windows or doors, or leaned
by fences to look at far scenes.
The surface of all weathered wood relaxed;
even gravel and cactus appeared soft.

The world had passed something in space
and was alone again. Sunset came on.
People lay down, and the birds forgot
as they sleepily clucked and slept, close
on boughs, as well hidden as could be
in the air again clear, sharp, and cold.

The Climb

One campfire higher every year
we hunt the height that made the wild men happy;
collecting all the wood we can
we huddle by the fire and sing
"Creeping Through the Needle's Eye."

Unless old knots can rouse the flame
through swirls and melt the snow that falls,
unless the cold can draw us higher
to learn by steeper flame how rich we are,
then we may starve; it's climb-or-famine time.

An Epiphany

You thinkers, prisoners of what will work:
a dog ran by me in the street one night,
its path met by its feet in quick unthought,
and I stopped in a sudden Christmas, purposeless,
a miracle without a proof, soon lost.

But I still call, "Here, Other, Other," in the dark.

Brevities

A Speech to the Birds:
    Sparrows, I'm lucky, too.

The Neighbor Who Came to Borrow Some Bread:
    In the clutter of the workbench I find
    my cup, the coffee just cool enough to drink.

Oedipus:
    At first he won so well he lost;
    then he lost so well he won.

August:
    Summer turns from is to was—
    acres of Queen Anne's lace.

The Rock on the Summit:
    Rain told it for years,
    and it has come to believe.

Evening News

That one great window puts forth
its own scene, the whole world
alive in glass. In it a war happens,
only an eighth of an inch thick.
Some of our friends have leaped
through, disappeared, become unknown
voices and rumors of crowds.

In our thick house, every evening
I turn from that world,
and room by room I walk, to
enjoy space. At the sink I start
a faucet; water from far is
immediate on my hand. I open our

door, to check where we live.
In the yard I pray birds,
wind, unscheduled grass,
that they please help to make
everything go deep again.

Humanities Lecture

Aristotle was a little man with
eyes like a lizard, and he found a streak
down the midst of things, a smooth place for his feet
much more important than the carved handles
on the coffins of the great.

He said you should put your hand out
at the time and place of need:
strength matters little, he said,
nor even speed.

His pupil, a king's son, died
at an early age. That Aristotle spoke of him
it is impossible to find—the youth was
notorious, a conqueror, a kid with a gang,
but even this Aristotle didn't ever say.

Around the farthest forest and along
all the bed of the sea, Aristotle studied
immediate, local ways. Many of which
were wrong. So he studied poetry.
There, in pity and fear, he found Man.

Many thinkers today, who stand low and grin,
have little use for anger or power, its palace
or its prison—
but quite a bit for that little man
with eyes like a lizard.

In Fur

They hurt no one. They rove the North.
Owning the wilderness, they're not lost.
They couple in joy; in fear, they run.
Old, their lives move still the same—
all a pattern across the land,
one step, one breath, one. . . .

Winter bundles them close; their fur
bunches together in friendly storms.
Everything cold can teach, they learn.
They stand together. The future comes.

Religion Back Home

1) When God's parachute failed,
   about the spring of 1945,
   the sky in Texas jerked open
   and we all sailed easily
   into this new strange harness on the stars.

2) The minister smoked,
   and he drank,
   and there was that woman in the choir,
   but what really finished him—
   he wore spats.

3) A Short Review of *Samson Agonistes*
   Written for Miss Arrington's Class
   in Liberal High School

   Our Father Who art in Heaven
   can lick their Father Who art in Heaven.

4) When my little brother chanted,
   "In 1492 Jesus crossed the ocean blue,"
   Mother said, "Bob, you mean
   Columbus crossed the ocean blue."
   And he said, "I always did get
   them two guys mixed up."

How I Escaped

A sign said "How to Be Wild—
the Lessons Are Free,"
so I edged past, bolted inside
carefully,
where the edge of a jaguar
roved beyond bars
and narrowed the room. Its head,
one eye at a time,
sewed the tent to the stars; and the cage
ballooned when he turned.

Mid-stride, I froze and stared
past enemies
that fell in droves down aisles
of my memories.
My bones—wild flowers—burned
at whatever I'd lost,
but my enemies burned up too
in that holocaust;
and I strode on, caged from them
in disregard,
swerving, momently aimed,
like a jaguar.

Though calm now, made to forgive
by bars between,
still fitted in those paw gloves
I walk what I mean.

186

IV

Mornings

1

Quiet,
rested, the brain begins to burn
and glow like a coal in the dark,
early—four in the morning, cold, with
frost on the lawn. The brain feels
the two directions of window, and as if
holding a taper, follows the hall
that leads to the living room and silver
space; lets the town come close, the chains
of lights turned off, and purposeless feet
of chairs sprawled; lets it all rise and
subside, and the brain pulses larger
than the ordinary horizon, but deliberately
less than it wants to go. All benevolence,
the brain with its insistent little call
summons wraiths and mist layers near
from fields: the world arising and streaming
through the house, soundless, pitifully
elongated, inevitable, for review, like breathing,
quiet.

2

Waiting
in the town that flows for the brain, charmed,
weak as distance, no one can move or belong
till the brain finds them and says, "Live!"
There's one too far, the phantom beyond the brain
each day that can't hear the kindest call
(and kindess is volume in the brain's room)—
the stranger with the sudden face, of
erased body, who floats into my dream
again. Down the storm our lack of storm

implies I hear the lambs cry, every one
lost and myself lost by where I made our
home. I feel a wind inside my hand.
By a lack that our life knows, life owns its greatness:
we are led one thing at a time through gain
to that pure gain—all that we lose. Stranger,
we are blind dancers in two different rooms;
we hear the music both heard long ago: wherever
you dance, that music finds you. When you turn,
I turn. Somewhere, whatever way you move
is ours; here, I keep our place,
repeat our turns, paced by my pulse,
waiting.

3

Lowly,
I listen as fur hears the air, and by will
I think one thing at a time while the world,
complete, turns—the farm where the wheat
votes, where they have already prayed the last day;
the glass of the ocean watching the storm;
all the extreme places; and I stand at the
prow of our house, an eye (for iris the attic window),
I gaze, and see so well my listening toes blur
on the rug and realize all the way to the island
of afternoon. My hands have given their gift,
then themselves. Can't the world see humility—my
trance, my face, the sober and steady spokes of my
bicycle? Many drive in piety and for the faith
an old car. Bishops in garages care, and presbyters
at the bank judge us—all that our shoes
and their crossed laces confess; angels behind
the counter inquire the name and send it up
the dizzying tube, and listen to the building
hum our estimation. Year by year the leaves
will come again, the suspicious grass, and the air
ever more tentative over the walls one color
at a time, fish of less than water, of evening;
shadows come and the bells get ready
before they sound, one part of a hum, like my self,
lowly.

188

4

Light
comes inside the brain. It is early;
in the attic I hear the wind lie down.
"Stay!" I call, as we tell the dog. Sudden as
the telephone, day says, "I am here!" And
in that clear light the brain comes home, lost
from all it wandered in, unable to be
sure for questioners, caught again by needs,
reduced to its trouble with my tongue.
The frank sycamore is at the window;
dark trails sink and go backward;
the sun comes over the world, aiming
the trees at the day, hill by hill.
Light.

Speculator

Treat the world as if it really existed.
Feel in the cold what hoods a mountain—
it is not your own cold, but the world's.
Distribute for the multitude this local discovery.

In flaws of wind in the beleaguered forest
where beaver eat their aspen food
hear every moved branch as the first breath of winter;
your window tree spells the same gray sky.

Make the moment go rich in your stammering,
the grape already on the tongue,
the words thought and old before they are said—
you can have time surrounded.

There is always a place like Now to be found:
at the edge of some Utah has to be some clay valley,
and you a placid witness of dinosaur bones.
You are foreign, part of some slow explosion.

189

Any Time

Vacation? Well, our children took our love apart:
"Why do you hold Daddy's hand?" "Susy's mother
doesn't have gray in her hair." And scenes crushed
our wonder—Sun Valley, Sawtooths, those reaches
of the Inland Passage, while the children took our
simple love apart.

(Children, how many colors does the light have?
Remember the wide shafts of sunlight, roads
through the trees, how light examines the road hour
by hour? It is all various, no simple on-off colors.
And love does not come riding west through the
trees to find you.)

"Daddy, tell me your best secret." (I have woven
a parachute out of everything broken; my scars
are my shield; and I jump, daylight or dark,
into any country, where as I descend I turn
native and stumble into terribly human speech
and wince recognition.)

"When you get old, how do you know what to do?"
(Waves will quiet, wind lull; and in that
instant I will have all the time in the world;
something deeper than birthdays will tell me all I need.)
"But will you do right?" (Children, children,
oh see that waterfall.)

Folk Song

First no sound, then you hear it—
so *Sally*, so *Tom*:
it is the past, its wisdom,
quick in the head again.

Back then when the moon climbed home
and someone began the song,
we were a people together
alive in the bush again.

Now, puzzle it with notes for a while,
shake it over the land:
this is your country, broken,
and broken and broken again.

Sing it together till you hold it—
all Sally, all Tom:
make our time, its promise,
come true in the air again.

Believing What I Know

A lake on the map of Canada
may forget in the snow—
in the spring be gone.

Imagine the flower-eyes
nodding a little breeze,
looking at the land where the lake was.

Many things that were true
disappeared, grew up in grass,
and now hide from flowers that stare.

I learn from the land. Some day
like a field I may take the next thing
so well that whatever is will be me.

Where We Are

Much travel moves mountains large
in your eyes—and then inside,
where those mountains climb the Everest
of all thought—tomorrows and maybes—
where expeditions often get lost.

Slow travel moves mountains best—
they pivot with dignity and bow
after you pass; they accompany
caravans for days, now and then
attacking, are driven back with snow.

We live in that cold range now
where the temporary earth tries
for something greater, with the keen air's aid,
and more, where the world perishes day
by day in the tall winter beyond any range.

Tragic Song

All still when summer is over
stand shocks in the field,
nothing left to whisper,
not even good-bye, to the wind.

After summer was over
we knew winter would come:
we knew silence would wait,
tall, patient, calm.

And that cold this winter gray wolves
deep in the North would cry
how summer that whispered all of us
at last whispers away.

At Our House

Home late, one lamp turned low,
crumpled pillow on the couch,
wet dishes in the sink (late snack),
in every child's room the checked,
slow, sure breath—

Suddenly in this doorway where I stand
in this house I see this place again,
this time the night as quiet, the house
as well secured, all breath but mine borne
gently on the air—

And where I stand, no one.

Allegiances

It is time for all the heroes to go home
if they have any, time for all of us common ones
to locate ourselves by the real things
we live by.

Far to the north, or indeed in any direction,
strange mountains and creatures have always lurked—
elves, goblins, trolls, and spiders:—we
encounter them in dread and wonder,

But once we have tasted far streams, touched the gold,
found some limit beyond the waterfall,
a season changes, and we come back, changed
but safe, quiet, grateful.

Suppose an insane wind holds all the hills
while strange beliefs whine at the traveler's ears,
we ordinary beings can cling to the earth and love
where we are, sturdy for common things.

Deerslayer's Campfire Talk

At thousands of places on any
mountain, exact rock faces lean
a strong-corner slant, balanced:
the whole country stays by such dependable
sets and shoulders—which endure unnoted.
    Bend after bend the river washes
its hands, never neglecting to kiss
every drop to every other—but that
is a small thing, not important.
    Tribes, or any traveling people,
will have some who stoke the fire
or carry the needed supplies—but
they take few great positions; hardly
anyone cares about them.

    Wherever I go they quote people
who talk too much, the ones who
do not care, just so they take the center
and call the plans.
    When I see these things, a part of my
mind goes quiet, and by a little turn
of my eyes I favor what helps, and ordinary
men, and that dim arch above us we seldom
regard, and—under us—the silent,
unnoted clasp of the rock.

In Fog

In fog a tree steps back.

Once gone, it joins those hordes
blizzards rage for over tundra.

With new respect I tell
my dreams to grant all claims;

Lavishly, my eyes close between
what they saw and that far flood

Inside: the universe that happens
deep and steadily.

In the Old Days

The wide field that was the rest of the world
came forward at evening, lowered
beyond our window shades; and Mother
spoke from her corner, about the wide field:

How someone whose eyes held another century
brought shadows of strange animals
over the mountains, and they were tethered
at night in little groups in the wide field,

And their eyes like wandering sparks
made constellations against the trees;
and how, many skies later, my father left
those animals and brought Mother news of the wide field.

Some time, some sunset, our window, she said,
would find itself again with a line of shadows
and the strange call would surround our house
and carry us away through the wide field.

Then Mother sang. But we listened, beyond:
we knew that the night she had put into a story was real.

Time

The years to come (empty boxcars
waiting on a siding while someone forgets
and the tall grass tickles their bellies)
will sometime stay, rusted still;
and a little boy who clambers up,
saved by his bare feet, will run
along the top, jump to the last car,
and gaze down at the end into that river
near every town.
                        Once when I was a boy
I took that kind of walk,
beyond the last houses, out where the grass
lived, then the tired siding where trains whistled.
The river was choked with old Chevies and Fords.
And that was the day the world ended.

Earth Dweller

It was all the clods at once become
precious; it was the barn, and the shed,
and the windmill, my hands, the crack
Arlie made in the axe handle: oh, let me stay
here humbly, forgotten, to rejoice in it all;
let the sun casually rise and set.
If I have not found the right place,
teach me; for, somewhere inside, the clods are
vaulted mansions, lines through the barn sing
for the saints forever, the shed and windmill
rear so glorious the sun shudders like a gong.

Now I know why people worship, carry around
magic emblems, wake up talking dreams
they teach to their children: the world speaks.
The world speaks everything to us.
It is our only friend.

196

These Days

Hurt people crawl as if they
suddenly love each part of themselves
again, after years of neglect,
as if the next place they might find
could bring a new sun in its hand,
or a mist they could separate and follow.

As if any time a bird might call and it
will be day, or from a ditch a cousin
or a lover will sing, hurt people
curiously turn their heads,
as if their duty, in a democracy, if
we are to have peace, is quickly
to crawl away over the horizon.

A Walk in the Country

To walk anywhere in the world, to live
now, to speak, to breathe a harmless
breath: what snowflake, even, may try
today so calm a life,
so mild a death?

Out in the country once,
walking the hollow night,
I felt a burden of silver come:
my back had caught moonlight
pouring through the trees like money.

That walk was late, though.
Late, I gently came into town,
and a terrible thing had happened:
the world, wide, unbearably bright,
had leaped on me. I carried mountains.

Though there was much I knew, though
kind people turned away,
I walked there ashamed—
into that still picture
to bring my fear and pain.

By dawn I felt all right;
my hair was covered with dew;
the light was bearable; the air
came still and cool.
And God had come back there
to carry the world again.

Since then, while over the world
the wind appeals events,
and people contend like fools,
like a stubborn tumbleweed I hold,
hold where I live, and look into every face:

Oh friends, where can one find a partner
for the long dance over the fields?

So Long

At least at night, a streetlight
is better than a star.
And better good shoes on a
long walk, than a good friend.

Often in winter with my old
cap I slip away into the gloom
like a happy fish, at home
with all I touch, at the level of love.

No one can surface till far,
far on, and all that we'll have
to love may be what's near
in the cold, even then.

198

Someday,
Maybe
1973

You know who you are:
This is for you, my friend.

I. Motorcycle, Count My Sins

An Introduction to Some Poems

Look: no one ever promised for sure
that we would sing. We have decided
to moan. In a strange dance that
we don't understand till we do it, we
have to carry on.

Just as in sleep you have to dream
the exact dream to round out your life,
so we have to live that dream into stories
and hold them close at you, close at the
edge we share, to be right.

We find it an awful thing to meet people,
serious or not, who have turned into vacant
effective people, so far lost that they
won't believe their own feelings
enough to follow them out.

The authentic is a line from one thing
along to the next; it interests us.
Strangely, it relates to what works,
but is not quite the same. It never
swerves for revenge,

Or profit, or fame: it holds
together something more than the world,
this line. And we are your wavery
efforts at following it. Are you coming?
Good: now it is time.

Thirteenth and Pennsylvania

Motorcycle, count my sins.
Pull away fast, drown them far.

Reverse my glance, blank windows; hold
sunset by the light in the sky.

Foot on the curb, reject what was.
By your thousands, people, absolve this man.

I glance my path into that deep frame
where wanderers plunge. I beg of the wind:

Read my lips, forget my name.

New Letters from Thomas Jefferson

Dear Sir:
   In Washington we are breathing very sincerely.

Very sincerely,
Thomas Jefferson

Dear Friend:
   I give you *The Faith of the Young*: Earlier generations were
more limited and selfish than the young generation. They polluted
the world, oppressed the weak, indulged hypocritically in alcohol
and food, flaunted their styles as superior (certain decorums in
dress and speech). Remnants of that generation can be identified
(besides by their age) by their callousness and arrogance. They
do not have interesting ideas or life styles or tastes. They are
cruel and dishonest. The governments they maintained or
tolerated were oppressive and corrupt.

Very sincerely,
Thomas Jefferson

My Friend, Dear Friend,

It is like the common wind that touches you by chance at your window, our stupendous coincidence: to be alive at the same time. Being contemporaries, having this common disability, we must endure together. I lift this day and carry it carefully west, lay it at your door. It is an instant heirloom so precious that the whole sky closes on its gray edge. Everything in the world has been caught in the scene we happen to share. Through all that calendar filigree stronger than steel I speak to you, on this island that is caving toward us all around, dear friend, my friend.

Yours,
Thomas Jefferson

George W., Sir:

This turn has become the way: wait when acting; add one further turn. Hidden by time there lives this extra advantage, coiled and elegant. Our choices now disguise, wait for what the world wants—old courtesy, new strategy. We follow by going ahead of what we know is coming.

By hand—
Thomas Jefferson

From Monticello

My Old Friend,

This morning the bees were swarming in the window well of the washroom. Birds were hunting each other. The root of the big yellow poplar was holding quiet as ever. Despite what we know and have done, I felt limited, alone. Across the morning light, particles were signaling what I cannot see.

As ever,
Thomas Jefferson

Glimpse Between Buildings

Now that the moon is out of a job
it has an easy climb, these nights,
finds an empty farm where a family could live,
slides wide over the forest—all those
million still violins before they are
carved—and follows those paths only air
ever uses. I feel my breath follow
those aisles and stumble on the moon
deep in forest pools. . . .

Moon, you old unsinkable submarine,
leaf admirer, be partly mine,
guide me tonight along city streets.
Help me do right.

For a Child Gone to Live in a Commune

Outside our ways you found
a way, no name for your home,
no number, not even words.

I thought your voice held onto curves
over cliffs when you said, "We let the animals
have whatever they wanted."

I forgot to tell you: this house too
is a wanderer. Under its paint it is
orbiting all I ever thought it would find—

Those empty spaces. It has found them.

Old Dog

Toward the last in the morning she could not
get up, even when I rattled her pan.
I helped her into the yard, but she stumbled
and fell. I knew it was time.

The last night a mist drifted over the fields.
In the morning she would not raise her head—
the far, clear mountains we had walked
surged back to mind.

We looked a slow bargain: our days together
were the ones we had already had.
I gave her something the vet had given,
and patted her still, a good last friend.

Hero

What if he came back, astounded
to find his name so honored, schools
named after him, a flame at his tomb,
his careless words cherished? How could
he ever face the people again, knowing
all he would know in that great clarity
of the other side? (His eyes flare into
the eyes of his wife. He searches his brothers'
drawn faces turned toward him suddenly still.)

No. Better abandoned in the ground,
recklessly cast back into the trash of
our atoms, all once loved let languish:
a lost civilization loses by particulars,
faith eroded by faithlessly treating
its servants. (Remember the slippering
progress the hearse made?—dwindling importantly
where faces could never really turn round?)

Our words apologize for such chill,
engulfing perspectives. We look deep into
the branded time helplessly and then come
chattering back for assurance, to shore up
our relics: *Arma virumque cano*. Such effort
it takes to build the high walls of Rome.

A Lecture on the Elegy

An elegy is really about the wilting of a flower,
the passing of the year, the falling of a stone.
Those people who go out, they just accompany
many things that leave us. Death is only
bad because it is like sunset, or a long eclipse.
If it had a dawn for company, or came with
spring, we would need laws to keep eager people
from rushing into danger and thus depopulating
        the world.

So, I have turned the occasion for such sadness
around: those graceful images that
seem to decorate the poems, they are
a rediscovery of those elements
that first created the obvious feelings,
the feelings that some people cannot even sense
until they are built up from little losses
and surrounded with labels: "war," "catastrophe,"
        "death."

That Time of Year

Remember T.J.?
His old car still chugs by at
night in the rain.

Sycamore leaves on
the lawn jump in the rain, let
go of October.

Sunsets kept up long
promises; now rain types out
slowly on the leaves:

"There   is   still   time."

A Girl Daddy Used to Know

Winter adopted her.
No form the hills can take
will ever solve that shape. When she
came in from her ranch along
the Cimarron to enroll at Liberal High
you could hear the boys' hearts kerplunk.

Her father was no one.
But once, seeing his hat in the
Saturday crowd, Daddy thought,
He sang her.

The people we choose are
the chosen people. But you look back,
you look back, and the stupid heart,
too dumb, too honest, never gets lost.

When Daddy's family moved away
the calendar wouldn't turn over.
For a long time the air he breathed
wouldn't let go of those hills.

World Staccato

Things that say clear, linger:
exact sounds mean the world is there—
the way a door clicks, that laconic
rifle we carried in bear country,
my camera that means eye intervals
exactly timed, and zips true,
the rock band that let its music
loose at the beat, then just before,
and that time we looked our message
across the room at each other—
"Are you the one?"—
and waited for the ping.

A Living

Even pain you can take, in waves:
call the interval happiness. You can
travel; whatever nags you, you can
change it. You can roll this burden away.
In the pinched bend of your street
you can look back, or ahead, or wait.

And there is easy talk, for throwing
back like Annie-Over, or a minuet,
a way to act human in these years the stars
look past. And somewhere around you begins
that lifted road lighted by sunset, offered
again and again, laced where the sky lives:

Someday your road.

Trying to Remember a Town

After our trip one town was lost;
it disappeared between Bergen and Oslo.
Daylight was flooding the valley and
apple blossoms were drowning.

We remember a flange of the sea, deep
mountains, and one of those cameos
that slip into your life sometimes—
this time a spiderweb touching a snail
crawling across a tombstone.

The town is gone; we are rich with it.
Now when bells redouble themselves
in the air, there is that instant:
the lost place lifts like a bubble.

Our blood makes a little leap over its name.

Waking at 3 A.M.

Even in the cave of the night when you
wake and are free and lonely,
neglected by others, discarded, loved only
by what doesn't matter—even in that
big room no one can see,
you push with your eyes till forever
comes in its twisted figure eight
and lies down in your head.

You think water in the river;
you think slower than the tide in
the grain of the wood; you become
a secret storehouse that saves the country,
so open and foolish and empty.

You look over all that the darkness
ripples across. More than has ever
been found comforts you. You open your
eyes in a vault that unlocks as fast
and as far as your thought can run.
A great snug wall goes around everything,
has always been there, will always
remain. It is a good world to be
lost in. It comforts you. It is
all right. And you sleep.

Love in the Country

We live like this: no one but
some of the owls awake, and of them
only near ones really awake.

In the rain yesterday, puddles
on the walk to the barn sounded their
quick little drinks.

The edge of the haymow, all
soaked in moonlight,
dreams out there like silver music.

Are there farms like this where
no one likes to live?
And the sky going everywhere?

While the earth breaks the soft horizon
eastward, we study how to deserve
what has already been given us.

Losing a Friend

Open the rain and go in,
close the gray door. Look
around. The whole world
is falling, and you are, and
all else outside the world falls.

In a shift of rain those faces
we once found come along.
They shine. Under the streetlight
they stay, all turned upward
where the gray door opens.

Out there flowers turn puppy faces
away from the wind. Even grass
learns how the world treats a friend.
Across prairies the terrible craving
pulls buffalo grass into far corners.

And at grasstop level over the calm
prairie a baby coyote stares. It is
teatime in Ottawa. On brick walls
a certain light begins to learn its way
up and across and over, touching words:

Day goes by. Gray door. No one. Save.

Some Days of Its Gift

It is a little day: no flags,
no guns flinging their caps,
and the Heads of State are too busy.
So it is our own holiday
like the others we take without
telling anyone else.

This whole day is your gift:
hold it and read a leaf at a
time, never hurried, never waiting.
Step, step, slide; then turn,
dance on the calendar,
reach out a hand, give lavish
as anyone ever gave—all.

Some days of its gift, no matter
how small, we say: "Thank you, Day."
I say it this day, Valentine.

Dreams to Have

1

They film a woman falling from a bridge
but the camera stops, and she stays
in the air. I remember that place
the rest of my life: it is going on
while events wait for their cues.

2

Time jerks its way forward and you are
a long-waiting part, ready, ready,
walking our town. I round your corner
and my eyes come true.

3

At a gallery every picture has us
in it: a frame back of the frame
pulls us, and I turn with an awkward
lope, heading outward. But that urge
takes me ever toward the center,
which moves.

4

A person mixing colors bends low
when we walk there. "Why are you
so intent on that bottle you are stirring?"
And then I know: in that little bottle
he has the sky.

The Escape

Now as we cross this white page together
people begin to notice us, and we
cut back and pretend indifference,
but all the time we pick up and lay
down our tracks cunningly, farther
and farther down the page. If we zig-
zagged or jumped a few times we could
make it, but even better would be
to take hands and perform a dance, our eyes
locked onto understanding, while our shadows
tell us which way to go. Those others
glare on our trail; they know what
is happening, and they certainly do not
approve. Remember, we are each other's: do not
look away. Every life is like this,
carried on while some inane plot
tries to intrude. How lucky we were
to find each other and make our escape
down the page and on out like this over the edge.

A Little Gift

Fur came near, night inside it,
four legs at a time, when the circus
walked off the train. From cage to cage
we carried night back to the cats and poured
it into their eyes, from ours. They
lapped steadily, and the sponge of their feet
swelled into the ground. Even today
I keep that gift: I let any next thing fold
quietly into the blackness that leads
all the way inward from the hole in my eye.

Three Looks out of a Window

1
Someone Went By

Someone went by in the alley
singing. The dogs trained their
ears and followed around a whole
arc of attention. In this air shell
each hermit carries his home.

We never know who it is.

2
Up in the Hills

Each place out of the wind has a name
so swift it escapes your lips when you
enter. You say it like the password God
already knows at His altar. But if
the spirit is wrong, then no matter how clear,

214

the word can't work. You go into each room
like that, naming it, humble: it sorts
itself out like the next look of your face.
Each room in the hills, they say,
belongs right where it is.

3
Lonesome

If you care, come by. We have
this place no one but a traveler sees.
And the only real traveler in a year
is the one in the leaves, inside the bundle
of leaves: the year itself. It says farewell
a million times, each time forever.

Hide and Go Seek at the Cemetery

Where snow can't find them
they hear us run across
their sky. They must hold
quiet, so very quiet, there.

With fingers crossed we cross
their field, and hide, and call
Come find me! Oh, I'm here!
I'm free! Not it! Not it!

They never move. No sound.
And then the snow.

In a Time of Need

We put our hands on the window—cold:
less of a world out there but more of its plain
hard shell. That scene is the still landscape
carved out of our days, a place time needed.

A time of need: we will drive over
the mountains. Whatever we find, it is
away from home. The years have drifted
wrong, and we are afraid, looking elsewhere.

Time to move—I walk through the empty house,
let the rooms flood still after me. I
pick up a picture. It curls, and the turning events
caught on the surface bend into themselves.

My still hand closes outside it, folds down while
the years flow together. I put the picture
into my mouth and run the long going away,
holding a calm face against the opening world.

Sleeping on the Sisters Land

Rain touches your face just at daylight.
No sky in the west: you turn your head
and the world revolves into gray so bright
that a glance like love falls deep
    toward the dreams that you left.

What lands are these, forever near?
They are great gray islands that come for us,
where the new dreams are, far as the sky
and the light, and sudden as rain
    that touches your face.

216

In the White Sky

Many things in the world have
already happened. You can
go back and tell about them.
They are part of what we
own as we speed along
through the white sky.

But many things in the world
haven't yet happened. You help
them by thinking and writing and acting.
Where they begin, you greet them
or stop them. You come along
and sustain the new things.

Once, in the white sky there was
a beginning, and I happened to notice
and almost glimpsed what to do,
But now I have come far
to here, and it is away back there.
Some days, I think about it.

Weeds

What's down in the earth
comes forth in cold water,
in mist at night, in muttering
volcanoes that ring oceans
moving strangely at times.

And in autumn all the fields
witness forth: power there
where roots find it, rooms
delved silently and left
for the dark to have.

Up and down all highways
weed flags proclaim,
"Great is Earth our home!"
as we slip our hand
into winter's again.

Great is Earth our home.
Great is the sky.
And great are weeds in the fields.
We celebrate earth and air
as we sing in the wind.

Room 000

After the last class in the empty room
chairs relax, each in a shadow,
and they all stand still and hear anti-lectures
all night long. Staccato silences
measure out the hours: "Where does the wind
end?" "What can the rain give?"
Standing around the absent students
those little whispers come near, nearer:
"Why is a hall? is a hall? is a hall?"

In a Museum in the Capital

Think of the shark's tiny brain
trapped in that senseless lust,
ripped through the tide, dismayed.

Think of The Great, helpless,
their very purposes caught
like ice that cannot be else.

And even The Wise are framed—
plans bound like a vise on the face,
and vanity roaring its claims.

The clock ticks on, every second
wandering down like a snowflake,
while an avalanche whispers our names.

Speaking Frankly

It isn't your claim, or mine, or
what we do or don't do, or how
we feel, or our gain or loss—it's something
other, and across our whole country a fine
soft rain comes, the wide gray clouds
and a sigh in the wind for us all.

Those endless experiments in woods and
grass go on, get ready to pay; the whole
world clenches itself, and quietly
shouts: it waves the days forward.
On the edge of each moment a little
voice tells the scenario, "Come."

And you feel it come down: the end,
the beginning, the part between, light
as a dance that draws near in the big
expanse maintained for us by the sky.
We go wandering out. And at the end we sense
here none of you, none of us—no one.

Existences

Half-wild, I hear a wolf,
half-tame, I bark. Then
in the dark I feel my master's
hand, and lick, then bite.

I envy leaves, their touch: miles
by the million, tongues everywhere
saying yea, for the forest,
and in the night, for us.

At caves in the desert, close
to rocks, I wait. I live
by grace of shadows. In moonlight
I hear a room open behind me.

At the last when you come
I am a track in the dust.

Friend

For anyone, for anyone,
the years are a sufficient storm:
over horizons in channels of wind
they blow, steady and long.

When I was young, when I was young,
I ran that storm—I walk it now.
And those who then companioned me,
save one, are gone.

They are nothing. They are nothing.
Forget them. What the sky can hold,
it holds, by day by day. But they—
they're lost, even on my inner sky.

From human loss, from gravel, from stone,
after years, one holds what one can.
I look out—that boy: undeterred,
he runs on through the withering world.

Father and Son

No sound—a spell—on, on out
where the wind went, our kite sent back
its thrill along the string that
sagged but sang and said, "I'm here!
I'm here!"—till broke somewhere,
gone years ago, but sailed forever clear
of earth. I hold—whatever tugs
the other end—I hold that string.

II. Wind World

Origins

So long ago that we weren't people then
our hands came upon this warm place on a rock
inside a high cave in the North, in the wilderness.
No light was there, but "Homeland" glowed in that dark
till time could carve it elsewhere with less force
in milder days, in the sun, far from the cold
where we crowded together around that promise and wailed.

Now along walls, over quilts, by locks, our hands
retell that story. Wherever touch finds hope again,
these hands remember that other time: they are lost;
they hunt for a place more precious than here.
Who will accept us wanderers? Where is our home?

Indian Caves in the Dry Country

These are some canyons
we might use again
sometime.

People of the South Wind

1

One day Sun found a new canyon.
It hid for miles and ran far away,
then it went under a mountain. Now Sun
goes over but knows it is there. And that
is why Sun shines—it is always looking.
Be like the sun.

2

Your breath has a little shape—
you can see it cold days. Well,
every day it is like that, even in summer.
Well, your breath goes, a whole
army of little shapes. They are living
in the woods now and are your friends.
When you die—well, you go with
your last breath and find the others.
And in open places in the woods
all of you are together and happy.

3

Sometimes if a man is evil his breath
runs away and hides from him. When he
dies his last breath cannot find the others,
and he never comes together again—
those little breaths, you know, in the autumn
they scurry the bushes before snow.
They never come back.

4

You know where the main river
runs—well, for five days below is
No One, and out in the desert
on each side his children live.
They have their tents that echo dust
and give a call for their father
when you knock for acquaintance:
"No One, No One, No One."

When you cross that land the sandbars
have his name in little tracks
the mice inscribe under the bushes,
and on pools you read his wide, bland
reply to all that you ask. You wake
from dreams and hear the end of things:
"No One, No One, No One."

Touches

Late, you can hear the stars. And beyond them
some kind of quiet other than silence, a deepness
the miles make, the way canyons
hold their miles back: you are in the earth and
it guides you; out where the sun comes
it is the precious world.

There are stones too quiet for these days,
old ones that belong in the earlier mountains.
You put a hand out in the dark of a cave and
the wall waits for your fingers. Cold, that stone
tells you all of the years that passed without knowing.
You think of caves held in the earth, no mouth,
no light. Down there the years have lost their way.
Under your hand it all steadies,
is the world under your hand.

Bring the North

Mushroom, Soft Ear, Old Memory,
Root Come to Tell the Air:
bring the Forest Floor along
the valley; bring all that comes
blue into passes, long shores
around a lake, talk, talk, talk,
miles, then deep. Bring that story.

Unfold a pack by someone's door—
wrapped in leather, brought in brown,
what the miles collect.
Leave sound in an empty
house in its own room there,
a little cube hung like a birdcage
in the attic, with a swinging door.
Search out a den: try natural,
no one's, your own, a dirt
floor. Accept them all.

One way to find your place is like
the rain, a million requests
for lodging, one that wins, finds
your cheek: you find your home,
a storm that walks the waves.
You hear that cloak whip, those
chilly hands take night apart.
In split Heaven you see one sudden
eye on yours, and yours in it,
scared, falling, fallen.

Mushroom, Soft Ear, Memory,
attend what is.
Bring the North.

The Airport at Anchorage

One plane, dragging its
foot, leans looking over
the fence by a prisonlike building.

All the planes look haggard and
scared: the land they fly over
won't even hold still for its
picture; it is always tugging
at itself, making new mountains.

Nimble in their boots, the people
try, but their world demands
so much that they are in debt
for fears, money, and promises.
(One of Baronof's trained natives
left a note by an unfinished job:
"We will finish this work yesterday.")

It is all in boxes, whatever
they have. They carry
wood, canvas, cardboard treasures
for the belly of the plane. They
snuggle in nearby and fly
away, after more boxes.

Report to Crazy Horse

All the Sioux were defeated. Our clan
got poor, but a few got richer.
They fought two wars. I did not
take part. No one remembers your vision
or even your real name. Now
the children go to town and like
loud music. I married a Christian.

225

Crazy Horse, it is not fair
to hide a new vision from you.
In our schools we are learning
to take aim when we talk, and we have
found out our enemies. They shift when
words do; they even change and hide
in every person. A teacher here says
hurt or scorned people are places
where real enemies hide. He says
we should not hurt or scorn anyone,
but help them. And I will tell you
in a brave way, the way Crazy Horse
talked: that teacher is right.

I will tell you a strange thing:
at the rodeo, close to the grandstand,
I saw a farm lady scared by a blown
piece of paper; and at that place
horses and policemen were no longer
frightening, but suffering faces were,
and the hunched-over backs of the old.

Crazy Horse, tell me if I am right:
these are the things we thought we were
doing something about.

In your life you saw many strange things,
and I will tell you another: now I salute
the white man's flag. But when I salute
I hold my hand alertly on the heartbeat
and remember all of us and how we depend
on a steady pulse together. There are those
who salute because they fear other flags
or mean to use ours to chase them:
I must not allow my part of saluting
to mean this. All of our promises,
our generous sayings to each other, our
honorable intentions—those I affirm
when I salute. At these times it is like
shutting my eyes and joining a religious
colony at prayer in the gray dawn
in the deep aisles of a church.

226

Now I have told you about new times.
Yes, I know others will report
different things. They have been caught
by weak ways. I tell you straight
the way it is now, and it is our way,
the way we were trying to find.

The chokecherries along our valley
still bear a bright fruit. There is good
pottery clay north of here. I remember
our old places. When I pass the Musselshell
I run my hand along those old grooves in the rock.

Sioux Haiku

On a relief map
mountains remind my fingers:
"Where Crazy Horse tried."

People with Whetstones

Hard-working hunters beyond the taiga
sharpen their knives, get up
early, watch carefully. They
have a name for everyone else:
"People who talk about God."

Stories to Live in the World with

1

A long rope of gray smoke was
coming out of the ground. I went
nearer and looked at it sideways.
I think there was a cave, and some people
were in a room by a fire in the earth.
One of them thought of a person like me
coming near but never quite coming in
to know them.

2

Once a man killed another, to rob him,
but found nothing, except that lying
there by a rock was a very sharp,
glittering little knife. The murderer
took the knife home and put it beside
his bed, and in the night he woke
and the knife was gone. But there was
no way for a person to get in to take the knife.

The man went to a wise old woman.
When she heard the story, she began to laugh.
The man got mad. He yelled at the woman
to tell why she was laughing. She looked
at him carefully with her eyes squinted
as if she looked at the sun. "Can't you
guess what happened?" she asked.

The man didn't want to be dumb; so
he thought and thought. "Maybe the knife
was so sharp that it fell on the ground
and just cut its way deeper and deeper and
got away." The woman squinted some more.
She shook her head. "You learned that from
a story. No, I will tell you why you
thought the knife was gone and why
you came here as ask me about it:
you are dead."

Then the man noticed that he didn't
have any shadow. He went out and
looked around: nothing had any shadow.
He began to squint up his eyes, it was
all so bright. And wherever he looked
there were sharp little knives.

This is a true story. He really was dead.
My mother told us about it. She told us
never to kill or rob.

3

At a little pond in the woods
I decided: this is the center of my life.
I threw a big stick far out, to be
all the burdens from earlier years.
Ever since, I have been walking
lightly, looking around, out of the woods.

Wind World

One time Wind World
found a way through the mountains
and called on Sky. Their
child was Thirst, who lives
wherever those two go, and brings
them ragged little dolls he
finds in the desert.

Wind World likes it near
the ground, and hurries there
even on still days, low.
You can see him shaking hands
with himself in the grass.

Wind World always made friends with
us Indians, who wore feathers for him.
Even today when he finds an arrowhead
in the dust or sand
he just leaves it there.

Wind World likes things that
move, but you notice
he has to pass something still
for him really to sing a song.

A Joshua tree near Mojave
told me these things one day
about Wind World.

Deer Stolen

Deer have stood around our house
at night so still nobody knew,
and waited with ears baling air.
I hunt the still deer everywhere,

For what they heard and took away,
stepping through the chaparral,
was the sound of Then; now it's Now,
and those small deer far in the wild

Are whispers of our former life.
The last print of some small deer's foot
might hold the way, might be a start
that means in ways beyond our ken

Important things. I follow them
through all the hush of long ago
to listen for what small deer know.

The Earth

When the earth doesn't shake, when the sky
is still, we feel something under the earth:
a shock of steadiness. When the storm is gone,
when the air passes, we feel our own
shudder—the terror of having such a great
friend, undeserved. Sometimes we wake
in the night: the millions better than we
who had to crawl away! We borrow their
breath, and the breath of the numberless
who never were born.

We know the motions of this great friend,
all resolved into one move, our stillness.
Why is no one on the hills where they
graze, the sun and the stars, no one
clamoring north, running as we would
run to belong to the earth? We come, we
celebrate with our breath, we join on the curve
of our street, never lost, the surge of the land
all around us that always is ours,
the beginning of the world and the end.

A Scene in the Country by a Telegraph Line

The father staggers to act it all out:
how heavy the load is, he says, that they
     do not understand.

"Look—wire opens its mouth; an operator leans in
and pours a jumble of letters, from anyone
     to anyone's friend."

By the pole where the wires hum, the little
brother leans. "Do you hear the letters, Bob?"
     "Yeah—some."

The sister doesn't want to look: people who
talk should always come near and help
   people they like.

They all gaze down a wire's mouth and hear
the mountain storm where the telegraph line
   shrills its life on and on.

The mother is not there. She is at home
to be where they can call, alone, together,
   or lost, or near, or far, any time.

Owl

An owl—the cold with eyes—
across where tribes endured
flew to mean winter
the way they did,
   the tribes.

A snowflake, even, could—
I mean could fly to stand
in much the same way
for all they did.
   They died,

No witness but the eyes,
no flake at large but wings,
no sound but the flow of stars,
and a claw of moon
   in the wood.

The eye of all that wood
—the owl that stares it all—
means the tribes are gone,
means winter, means
   the claw.

And moonset means our star.

232

The Widow Who Taught at an Army School

She planted bullets in a window box,
lead tips up like a row of buds,
and she told the children: "Every charge
the Indians made was a dance for their horses,
but serious men made the Gatling gun;
its bullets come true forever—you go
mad from shooting the gun.

"From east of the mountains, from Daylight Lake,
morning begins," she said,
"and it loves us all; its edge opens the field.
Children, let's sing 'Rescue Me, Day,'
for we are all prisoners here."

There are widows like that in many schools,
and officers with eyes like badges
that follow a look past the window box,
ready for a dance but mad from the gun,
and stare out over the field.

The Lost Meteorite in the Coast Range

No foot comes here, where
my eye looks up through
grass. This hidden stream
and its long border
belong to the clouds, and
they watch me for their own.
I hold a deep, rich quiet,
falling forever around the sun
through the still sky.

233

The Little Ways That Encourage Good Fortune

Wisdom is having things right in your life
and knowing why.
If you do not have things right in your life
you will be overwhelmed:
you may be heroic, but you will not be wise.
If you have things right in your life
but do not know why,
you are just lucky, and you will not move
in the little ways that encourage good fortune.

The saddest are those not right in their lives
who are acting to make things right for others:
they act only from the self—
and that self will never be right:
no luck, no help, no wisdom.

Crossing the Desert

Little animals call
us, tiny feet whisper, and
a certain wide wing shadow
flickers down the gray wind
over the sage.

Pardon! Pardon!—
a ditch at night is a church
where eyes burn candles, mile after
silent mile, whatever comes,
whatever comes.

Every time the world comes
true, they cry from the ditch,
our cousins offering their paws,
a light hanging in their eyes,
returning our own.

234

After That Sound, After That Sight

After that sound we weren't people
any more. It came in the night.
It froze all other sound. We are
afraid to listen any more.
After that sight there was hurt
in every eye. Animals have
that look, a memory that seeing
will never make fade.

I walk the world; the day
falls warm, then thinned.
Whatever we passed, a sky
out there swallowed our sky.
From somewhere else began
a new part of time.

Journey

You ramble over the wilderness, a bear or
a wolf, on the left a friend,
on the right one to watch. Eyes
give each other their flame and go out
when you meet. There was an event
so great that you study each other, but
so long ago that your shoulders forget
in a rain where later things grow.
You ramble home. What happened?
Nothing. But you study the floor.
Should you say, "I was a bear or
a wolf"? No, you can't.
But you were.

The Whole Story

1

When we shuddered and took into ourselves
the cost of the way we had lived,
I was a victim, touched by the blast.
Death! I have death in me!
No one will take me in from the cold.

Now among leaves I approach, and I
am afraid that pain and anger
have crept their fire into my bones,
but the slaver around my mouth is drying.
I hope that the light on the hills can
pass open woods and slide
easily around slopes, hold my eyes
before they search their way to an enemy:
I have to contain all this anger, but with luck
it can pass directly into the sky.

2

I am the sky. After everything ends
and even while the story goes on
I accept all that is left over. When all
the signals finally die, they still find
their way everywhere, meaning the same
as ever: they can't get away. I hold
them for something that approaches through winter.

3

Though I am winter, through the light on the hills
I let children approach. In a pale straw slant
the sun angles down. Maybe the children will not see
the victims, will somehow survive. The sun touches
along and goes away, and while the stars
come out the sky waits and wherever they look
it is now and there is still time.

236

4

I am time. When you look up
from this page I will be waiting to go
with you to the end of the story.

III. Report from a Far Place

In the Desert

What is that stiff figure
moving oddly out in the sun alone?
Why does it not run, stoop, go
where the wind invites, be free?

Stranger, I am that figure.
My actions only a long life can
explain. I have lived years in a space
divided by unseen cut and pain.

Many little things I do in this
long, dry land to be freed. I ration
small acts of honesty, to use like
salt pills, one at a time, at need.

For some I know, things are better,
they say. They live with what
comes. If they like something
they move near, if not they go away.

Out here I stand, a thousand hurts
remembered in every move. I do
a strange dance, but I drink the company
of those who are unafraid.

And now and then, like this,
I hold up my hand for shade.

The Moment

It happens lonely—no one,
then sky. Where is it?
Yorkshire? Wyoming? It doesn't
matter: lonely. Tremendous.
Anywhere. Suddenly.

Is it just you, Wind?
Maybe. But it is Now;
it is what happens, the moment,
the stare of the moon, an
opening birds call out of,
anything true. We have it.

That's what the rich old
shepherd meant, pointing
through the storm at
the blowing past wind
passing nothing:
"Those who have gone
and those who never existed,
they don't have it."

The Swerve

Halfway across a bridge one night
my father's car went blind. He guided
it on by no star but a light he kept in mind.

Halfway to here, my father died.
He looked at me. He closed his eyes.
The world stayed still. Today I hold in mind

The things he said, my children's lives—
any light. Oh, any light.

238

Report from a Far Place

Making these word things to
step on across the world, I
could call them snowshoes.

They creak, sag, bend, but
hold, over the great deep cold,
and they turn up at the toes.

In war or city or camp
they could save your life;
you can muse them by the fire.

Be careful, though: they
burn, or don't burn, in their own
strange way, when you say them.

Freedom

Freedom is not following a river.
Freedom is following a river,
    though, if you want to.
It is deciding now by what happens now.
It is knowing that luck makes a difference.

No leader is free; no follower is free—
    the rest of us can often be free.
Most of the world are living by
creeds too odd, chancy, and habit-forming
    to be worth arguing about by reason.

If you are oppressed, wake up about
four in the morning: most places,
you can usually be free some of the time
    if you wake up before other people.

The Little Lost Orphans

Leaves took them in, lost
them, numbering along through summer
and the wind. Reading their story, I follow
those leaf hands, and every vein guides
fate. I agree with all that happens
at the end: right, right, right.

No other guide but *is*
leads onward, then disappears after persuading
my look. But even today when I trace the right
leaf, the real world I have earned
falls upward, and I lie again on the ground,
hands curled for orphans and all their tomorrows.

The Eskimo National Anthem

Wherever I work, some vibration
in the machinery or some fluting corner
that catches the wind will start up
again the Eskimo national anthem,
   Al-eena, Al-wona.

That song we heard, "Somebody, Maybe,"
has drawn into its lines most
of the world. Like a drop of oil
the sound slowly thins outward,
   Al-eena, Al-wona.

I keep looking for that early morning
beyond a wall when a man first passed
whistling that song. It was easy to
go back to sleep, and the moment got away,
   Al-eena, Al-wona.

Now while the boss talks or while an official
tells me what to do, the bears at Talkeetna
begin to dance, and the escaping files of
birch trees make it away over the pass,
    Al-eena, Al-wona.

If my life never amounts to anything,
if what I intended never gets done,
that song may be to blame. On the other
hand, it is a kind of a comfort,
    Al-eena, Al-wona.

People Who Went by in Winter

The morning man came in to report
that something had crossed the field
in the night during the storm. He heard
ribbons of wind snap at their tether
and a sound like some rider saying
the ritual for help, a chant or a song.
When we went out all we found
were deep, slow tracks in freezing mud
and some sticks tied together hanging
from the lowest branch of the oldest
tree by the river.

While beginning snow eddied and curtained
thicker and thicker on, we looked.
The grass hurried by, seething, then silent,
brown, all the way to the west, a little
touch-by-touch trail to the mountains.
Our boss turned back: "No.
We can't help them. They sing till
they find a place to winter. They have
tents. They make it, somehow." He
looked off that long way, where
the grass tossed.

Riding home, he told us:
"My people were like them,
over around Grand Prairie—slaves once,
then landowners. Now they pass like
this, and I hear them, because
I wake up and am partly theirs."
He looked at every man, and
he put his hand on the neck of his horse:
"They are our people, yours and mine,
all of us," he said.
"In every storm I hear them pass."

Witness

This is the hand I dipped in the Missouri
above Council Bluffs and found the springs.
All through the days of my life I escort
this hand. Where would the Missouri
meet a kinder friend?

On top of Fort Rock in the sun I spread
these fingers to hold the world in the wind;
along that cliff, in that old cave
where men used to live, I grubbed in the dirt
for those cool springs again.

Summits in the Rockies received this diplomat.
Brush that concealed the lost children yielded
them to this hand. Even on the last morning
when we all tremble and lose, I will reach
carefully, eagerly through that rain, at the end—

Toward whatever is there, with this loyal hand.

Now

Where we live, the teakettle whistles out
its heart. Fern arrives to
batter the window. Every day gets lost
in a stray sunset and little touches of air.
Someone opens a door. It is this year.

We hear crickets compute their brittle
almanac. A friend or a stranger
comes to the door; it is always "Hello" again,
but just a friend or a stranger.
We get up and look out: a good year?

God knows. People we meet look older.
They ask how we are. It is this year.

Our Time's Name

Uncle Relevant has
moved into the living room. His
muddy boots mark the furniture.

The children stop and look at
the great guest. They hear the keys
in his pockets: Riches, Power, Death.

"The first thing you think every morning,"
Uncle Relevant says, "is that day's first name.
And the last thing is that day's epitaph."

Running past the window, neighbor kids
play sticking out their tongues.
Around them the whole world
   breathes all the time.

Blackberries Are Back

Blackberries are back. They cling near
little streams. Their eyes, bright mornings,
make tunnels through the vines.
They see their own thorns in the sky,
and the print of leaves.

At night they hide inside the wind,
ready to try the outdoors on.
They swing for distance, root for
fidelity. The truth is your only ransom
once they touch your tongue.

Composed, Composed

The flat people in magazines hear
the flat god of their tabletop say,
"Let there be flat people," and
there are ads and editorials.

The tall people in sport have their own
say: "Winning is right;
I wouldn't want to be short."
God still says,
"Let there be light."

A Song in the Manner of Flannery O'Connor

Snow on the mountain—water in
the valley: you beat a mule and
it works hard, Honey.
   Have a cigarette?

Where is the guidepost? Written on
your hand: you point places with it
and everyone understands.
     Like to dance, Honey?

Country folks used to talk to us
like this. Now they're wiser
than the rest of us.
     So long, Sucker.

Have You Heard This One?

A woman forged her face.
(It was one she found in a magazine.)
Using it, she got a job on an airline.
One day a passenger said, "Haven't I seen
you everyplace before?" (He had been reading
Ring Lardner.) They got married
that very night in a motel.

This is a true story.
It happened in New York
and Los Angeles
and Chicago
and . . .

Ozymandias's Brother

Without the style of Ozymandias, therefore
needing less (he hardly has a tomb), a brother
lived up the canyon. His words can't be deciphered,
an unknown code, but I know what they are,
from being the same kind of brother—
that's one way to know.

Or—say a bird found that little stone;
no one else ever saw it: carved
words in an unknown language, shallow letters—
He was here for a while, then gone. That's
about the right degree of assertion, holding forth
what there is, no despair.

I'd put them on my tomb the same;
so I read them by half them and half *me*.
He was here, didn't have much, died
without any mighty works, no honor,
not much in the bank for the stonecutter.
Here's what I think it says:

"Anyway, it was the world."

Juncos

They operate from elsewhere,
some hall in the mountains—
quick visit, gone.
Specialists on branch ends,
craft union. I like their
clean little coveralls.

Dear Mother

1

Inside this camera I am tied to the film,
facing the opposite wall, I think, where
waits the lens. The whole room I am in
swings around and stops. In a minute
a stab of twisted light will click and
part of the world will leap into my head.

2

Now I am tied to the needle of a record
player. Grooves curve nearer and nearer
under my feet. In a sudden shudder that
longitudinally sweeps creation into a beat
soon I will be exactly trained and swept
along one whole day's production by Bach.

3

Wait! Let me go! I am hid inside a new bomb
nestled in the belly of our oldest craft, The Whale,
submerged off the Sea of Japan. Swaddled and
warm, enriched with oxygen, I am
to zip ashore tomorrow unrolling a cord
and appear, benevolent, speaking Korean.

4

Later, woven into the magazines, I will
find a place. But, Mother, where can you forward
my mail? Put it in a bottle marked for me,
or ask a computer which of its cousins could find
your boy, for I am to start a series tomorrow for
The Times, Listen, and the *Ladies' Home Journal.*

I won't be home for a while.

The Stick in the Forest

A stick in the forest that pointed
where the center of the universe is
broke in the wind that started
its exact note of mourning
when Buddha's mother died.

Around us then a new crystal
began to form itself, and men—
awakened by what happened—
held precious whatever breathed:
we are all gestures that the world makes.

"Be, be," Buddha said.

For the Governor

Heartbeat by heartbeat our governor tours
the state, and before a word and after a word
over the crowd the world speaks to him,
thin as a wire. And he knows inside
each word, too, that anyone says,
another word lurks, and inside that . . .

Sometimes we fear for him: he, or someone,
must act for us all. Across our space
we watch him while the country leans
on him: he bears time's tall demand,
and beyond our state he must think the shore
and beyond that the waves and the miles and
    the waves.

Vespers

As the living pass, they bow
till they imitate stones.
In the steep mountains then
those millions remind us:
    every fist the wind has
    loses against those faces.

And at the end of the day
when every rock on the west
claims a fragment of sun,
a last bird comes, wing and
   then wing over the valley
   and over the valley, and home,

Till unbound by our past we sing
wherever we go, ready or not,
stillness above and below, the slowed
evening carried in prayer toward the end.
   You know who you are:
   This is for you, my friend.

Indexes

Index of Titles

Index of First Lines

Both sides fought stillness   175
Breaking every law except the one   121
Brown in the snow, a car with a heater   162
By footworn boards, by steps   73
By the secret that holds the forest up   74

Calmly through the bars observe   77
Cedars darkened their slow way   32
Clouds on the hills. I hear a throat voice   160
Cold nights outside the taverns in Wyoming   9
Crisis they call it?—when   81

Dandelion cavalry, light little saviors   14
Day after day up there beating my wings   77
Deaf to process, alive only to ends   55
Dear Governor   171
Dear ones, watching us on any street   134
Dear Sir   202
Deer have stood around our house   230
Dogs that eat fish edging tidewater die—   41
"Don't you want people to think well of you?"   136
Downhill, any gait will serve   12
Down in the Frantic Mountains   35
Downstream they have killed the river and built a dam   43

Early in March we pitched our scar   127
Evening came, a paw, to the gray hut by the river   85
Even in the cave of the night when you   209
Even pain you can take, in waves   208
Even the flaws were good—   130
Every lamp that approves its foot   154

Falling separate into the dark   86
Far as the night goes, brittle as the stars   40
First no sound, then you hear it—   190
First the falls, then the cave   166
First the soul of our house left, up the chimney   71
For anyone, for anyone   220
For years I was tuned a few notes too high—   15
Freedom is not following a river   239
Frightened at the slant of the writing, I looked up   130
From all encounters vintages ensue   92
From my head this bubble labeled "Love"   10
From old Fort Walla Walla and the Klickitats   37
Fur came near, night inside it   214

Girl in the front row who had no mother   83
God is never sure He has found   138
Good things will happen   95
Grass that was moving found all shades of brown   16
Guitar string is   11

Halfway across a bridge one night   238
Half-wild, I hear a wolf   220

262

About the Author

WILLIAM STAFFORD was born in Hutchinson, Kansas, in 1914, and studied at the University of Kansas and the University of Iowa, where he received his doctorate. At intervals during his schooling, he worked as a laborer in sugar beet fields, on construction jobs, and in an oil refinery. During World War II he worked in alternative service as a conscientious objector for four years, in Forest Service and Soil Conservation camps, going on to serve with The Brethren Service Commission and Church World Service.

Mr. Stafford has taught high school in California and in colleges and universities in California, Alaska, Indiana, Kansas, Washington, Ohio and Oregon. He has been on the faculty of Lewis and Clark College in Portland, Oregon, since 1948, where he is professor of English.

His poems have appeared in many magazines since the 1950s, in the United States and abroad and have been anthologized widely. They have brought him honorary degrees and awards, including the National Book Award for Poetry for his volume *Traveling Through the Dark* (1962). He served as Consultant in Poetry for the Library of Congress in 1970–71. He and his wife, parents of four, live in Lake Oswego, Oregon.